GOD IS WITH Us

How We HEAR HIM

PRAISE FOR *GOD IS WITH US*

"Never has the world needed to 'hear Him' more than right now. This beautiful book and its powerful stories arrived at the perfect time in my life—and perhaps in yours."

—JASON F. WRIGHT

New York Times, Wall Street Journal, and *USA Today* bestselling author

"If you are struggling to find answers, overcome a difficult problem, or obtain relief in a heartbreaking world, this is a balm in Gilead. When your burdens seems heavy and solutions seem few, *God Is with Us: How We Hear Him* will lift you up—turning your heart to the Master Healer, from whom all grace flows. Open these pages and find in it the peace you seek."

—ANGELA ESCHLER

Editor, entrepreneur, and author of women's inspirational nonfiction

"Real, personal, and powerful. The prophet has asked us to better 'hear Him,' and this book shares in-the-trenches ways to make it happen. Poignant stories and real-time triumphs inspire the desire to make hearing Him a priority anytime, anywhere, in any situation."

—CONNIE SOKOL

Founder of Disciple Thought Leaders, bestselling author, speaker, and TV contributor

"What a beautiful book full of faith-inspiring stories! Rather than delve into the doctrinal details of what it means to 'hear Him,' the Hepplers teach in the way most people learn best—through stories. And what a collection they've compiled! From both men and women, the young and the old, these experiences wonderfully illuminate what it's like to receive personal revelation in real-life scenarios. Whether you're facing simple trials or a devastating tragedy—or just want to hear God's voice better—you'll find plenty in this book to help you in your lifelong quest to 'hear Him.'"

—LIZ KAZANDZHY

Author of *The Holy Ghost from A to Z: What the Spirit Can Do for You*

GOD
IS WITH *Us*

How We HEAR HIM

DIONY & TRENT HEPPLER

CFI
An imprint of Cedar Fort, Inc.
Springville, Utah

ISBN 13: 978-1-4621-4417-4

Published by CFI, an imprint of Cedar Fort, Inc.
2373 W. 700 S., Suite 100, Springville, UT 84663
Distributed by Cedar Fort, Inc., www.cedarfort.com

Library of Congress Control Number: 2022946548

Cover design by Courtney Proby
Cover design © 2023 Cedar Fort, Inc.
Edited and typeset by Liz Kazandzhy

Printed in the United States of America

10 9 8 7 6 5 4 3 2 1

Printed on acid-free paper

DEDICATION

*To all those who are striving
every day to hear Him.*

Other Books by Diony Heppler

Torn Apart

Imperfectly Beautiful

A Sisterhood of Strength

Heaven's Just a Prayer Away

Other Books by Trent Heppler

The Power Within

ACKNOWLEDGMENTS

Writing this book was an experience in "hearing Him." From the moment the idea first entered our minds to the moment we typed the final sentence, He led us along, giving us multiple spiritual impressions on how to proceed, what to include, who to ask to contribute, and how to put it all together. Our hearts are drawn out in humility and gratitude for His guiding hand in our daily lives and for this chance to publicly say, through the written word, "God is with us."

We offer special thanks to all who bravely shared their personal and often sacred stories, including those who requested to remain anonymous: Michelle S. Badger, Wendy L. Bangerter, Erica Banks, Rosemary Bennett, John and Pam Bolla, Heidi Bennett-Checketts, Lori Conger, Corrine Frazier, Merada Gregory, Amanda Hayes, Kathy Hirschi, Megan Hirschi, Brock Josephson, David King, Marjorie, Meghan, Robert Mayo, Teri McCown, Tami Myers, Cher Park, Brian and Priscilla Price, Rachel Scott, Elaine Stinnett, Matthew Taylor, Daniel Turner, Todd, Shelby Salazar, and John Wilcox.

It is our prayer that, through sharing, we will all hear Him more clearly and more often!

CONTENTS

CONTENTS

CONTENTS

Preface

Fear
By Diony

Four months before my eighth birthday, my father left our home in Anchorage, Alaska, to go on a fly-in caribou hunting trip with two friends in a nearby national park.

I never saw him again.

On the return trip, visibility was good, but the cloud ceiling had dropped below the tops of the mountains to the north and south of the entrance to Merrill Pass, his intended route home. If the pass closed before he made it through, the plan was for him to turn around.

Five long days passed unmercifully slow as we wondered, cried, hoped, and prayed that my dad was safely holed up in a cabin somewhere. On the afternoon of the sixth day, I walked home from the bus stop after school with my two brothers, swinging my empty lunch box in one hand, occasionally brushing a lock of auburn hair off my chilled-rosy cheek with the other. Our silence was companionable, shaded within the myriad of our own thoughts.

When my house came into view, any contemplative emotions of the earlier day were rapidly swept away with surprise. Both sides of the street in front of our home were lined with unfamiliar cars.

The large pine tree in the front yard still stood tall, its towering branches filtering the cold, cloudless, early spring sky. Drifts of snow still dotted the edges of our steep sloping driveway and the lawns of neighboring homes. A well-used snow shovel still leaned against the garage side wall. All was as it was when I'd left that very morning, but now something felt different.

A dog barked in the background, the sound barely registering as I picked up my pace. I bounded toward the front door, came inside, and raced upstairs.

"Mom, where are—" I called as I entered the kitchen. The last word of my searching phrase caught in the back of my throat as my blue eyes scanned a crowd of people. None of them were her.

I froze, catching my breath, my cheeks growing hot. Off to the right, someone moved and then touched my shoulder. I pulled away feeling uncertain, but then I recognized her as a close family friend. She nudged me in the direction of the living room.

With my brothers close behind, I finally found my mom. She was sitting in my dad's La-Z-Boy recliner—an unfamiliar scene. Her face was pale but composed, yet I could tell she had been crying.

My heart was pounding.

She reached out to me, putting her arm around me to draw me close. She smelled good—comfortingly familiar—and for a second I relaxed in her warmth, briefly putting my head on her shoulder. But soon my other four siblings crowded in, and I felt her body shift. I was vaguely aware of others in the room with us, clustered in small groups talking softly. As soon as my siblings and I surrounded her, as if on cue, the voices stopped. All went silent, holding their breath expectantly for the elephant in the room to be addressed.

My brave mother let it out.

She told us our father never made it to the pass. His Piper PA-12 aircraft didn't clear the tops of those nearby mountains. The search and rescue team had found the wreckage that morning about forty-eight miles northwest of Port Alsworth. My father and his friend had both died on impact.

As the tears poured from all of our eyes, my brain refused to comprehend the fact that *my* father would never be coming home. Disbelief and shock rocked my world. How could *my* father be dead? How could that have happened to *me*?

The days that followed turned into weeks and then months. On the outside, I lived in the same house, on the same street, with the same people. I had the same friends, I went to the same school and church, and I ate the same things. My daily routine continued. But on the inside, my father's absence changed everything for me. My world no longer felt safe. Life had become a big question mark. If I had unexpectedly lost my father, what would (or could) happen next? My heart became heavy with fear—a new feeling for me.

The painfully difficult challenge of losing my father at such a young age greatly impacted my life, teaching me many things. Most importantly, it was the beginning of my faith journey that continues to this day—a journey of relying on God in everything and learning how to *hear Him*. It was a beginning—learning that no matter what happened, I could turn to Him and He would always be there.

Darkness
By Trent

As I lay in bed, I had an overwhelming feeling of darkness surround me. Fear—no, *terror*—pierced my soul. I was hot and cold at the same time. I felt like I couldn't catch my breath. Satan had unleashed as many dark spirits on me as he could. I did the only thing I could think of: I sat up on the lower bunk of my bed in the missionary training center, raised my arm in the air, and commanded Satan to depart in the name of the Lord Jesus Christ. I had heard people tell stories of how doing that could work, but I didn't know. There was a lot I didn't know.

I didn't know if I believed in the Book of Mormon. I didn't know for certain if The Church of Jesus Christ of Latter-day Saints was true. I had been set apart as a missionary to serve for two years of my life, and now I was beginning it without having had a spiritual witness of the doctrines I had committed to preach.

Satan must have known this.

I had grown up in the Church and was baptized at age eight. I attended every week, participated in Boy Scouts and mutual, graduated from seminary, and had given many talks. I thought I knew the Church was true, but I had never received a clear answer that it was—because I had never prayed to ask.

It would have made sense that before deciding, submitting, interviewing, opening the call, and then leaving on a mission to a foreign land that I would have prayed about it. However, from a young age, I had always just planned on going. That was what was done and expected, and I didn't like to disappoint.

I was the youngest in a large family, with a ten-year gap between me and my oldest sibling and five more siblings in between. Physically I was different. All my older siblings were either athletes or cheerleaders, but I struggled with being overweight. I developed a personality of not wanting to ever disappoint those who loved me because I was already disappointed enough in myself for being obese. A large part of my identity came from church. I enjoyed going, and I had made many good friends there—"church" was just who we were. I had been taught about Jesus Christ, and on that night in the missionary training center, overcome with feelings of dark despair, I called on Him.

Immediately the crushing weight was taken from my body, mind, and soul. The darkness lifted, and I felt sweet, quiet, flowing energy radiate throughout my entire being. It was peace, hope, joy, love, and truth. I was feeling the Spirit for the first time. I was *hearing Him*. I crawled out of bed, fell to my knees, and had my first conversation with my Father in Heaven. Not a prayer—a conversation. I thanked Him for the miracle of releasing me from the devil. I asked Him if the Book of Mormon was true, and the same amazing energy flowed through me again. It was true—and now I knew that for myself.

This was the first time I truly heard Him. I knew at that moment that I wanted others to feel the same amazing, truth-defining, peace-giving internal compass that I had felt.

Since that experience thirty years ago, I have lived a life of challenges that have refined my understanding of how to hear Him. These trials have multiplied a hundredfold the love I feel for my Savior Jesus Christ. They have helped me to know Him better and choose Him more every day. They have made me want to align my purpose with His in whatever He has planned for me.

Choosing this path has often felt like the "hard road," with pain and challenges arising from each new experience. But isn't this the reason we are here on this earth? Like my favorite scripture states, God sent His children here to "prove them herewith, to see if they will do all things whatsoever the Lord their God shall command them" (Abraham 3:25).

The suffering and triumphs I felt during that experience in the missionary training center were an awakening, giving me better insight into hearing Him.

INTRODUCTION
LEARN TO HEAR HIM

"Behold, a virgin shall be with child, and shall bring forth a son, and they shall call his name Emmanual, which being interpreted is, God with us."
Matthew 1:23

We can hear the Lord in many ways, during every season of our lives, if we focus and tune in to how He lets us know He is there. The inspiring true stories contained in this book—collected from dozens of individuals—illustrate this truth.

President Russell M. Nelson said, "We are living in a remarkable age when we constantly see the hand of the Lord in the lives of His children. Our Heavenly Father and His Son Jesus Christ know us, love us, and are watching over us. Of that we can be certain."[1] "When we seek to hear—truly hear—His Son [Jesus Christ], we will be guided to know what to do in any circumstance."[2]

Here are some of the many ways we can hear Him.

The scriptures teach us how to find Him, feel Him, and receive His help.

"Search the scriptures . . . they are they which testify of me" (John 5:39). When we set aside time each day to study God's word, we can more readily hear Him as our knowledge about Him and His ways increases. We are promised, "If any of you lack wisdom, let him ask of God, that giveth to all men liberally, and upbraideth not; and it shall be given him" (James 1:5). And as we "seek, [we] shall find" (Matthew 7:7).

Hearing Him can occur through the Holy Ghost when we slow down, push away distractions, and start listening more with our hearts than with our ears.

We need to "be still and know that [He is] God" (Doctrine and Covenants 101:16), having faith He will answer and guide us in His time and in His way. As we practice recognizing the promptings of the Holy Ghost, we become better at discerning the ways He speaks to us. If we are "expecting the spectacular, [we] may not be fully alerted to the constant flow of revealed communication"[3] because He often speaks to us quietly, subtly, and in small ways.

Answers can come to our minds and our hearts in the form of impressions, thoughts, and feelings. "I will impart unto you of my Spirit, which shall enlighten your mind" (Doctrine and Covenants 11:13). "Yea, behold, I will tell you in your mind and in your heart, by the Holy Ghost, which shall come upon you and dwell in your heart. Now, behold, this is the spirit of revelation" (Doctrine and Covenants 8:2–3).

"These delicate, refined spiritual communications are not seen with our eyes, nor heard with our ears. And even though it [may be] described as a voice, it is a voice that one feels, more than one hears. . . . The Spirit does not get our attention by shouting or shaking us with a heavy hand. Rather, it whispers. It caresses so gently that if we are preoccupied we may not feel it at all. . . . Occasionally it will press just firmly enough for us to pay heed. But most of the time, if we do not heed the gentle feeling, the Spirit will withdraw and wait until we come seeking and listening."[4]

The pattern of receiving promptings was taught by the Savior. The Apostle John witnessed that the Lord "received not of the fulness at first, but continued from grace to grace, until he received a fulness" (Doctrine and Covenants 93:13). Over time, the Lord teaches us the things we should know, allowing us the chance to grow and develop our faith in Him. "I will give unto the children of men line upon line, precept upon precept, here a little and there a little; and blessed are those who hearken unto my precepts, and lend an ear unto my counsel, for they shall learn wisdom" (2 Nephi 28:30).

Hearing Him can bring an increase of light, knowledge, and understanding.

"That which is of God is light" (Doctrine and Covenants 50:24). The Prophet Joseph Smith taught, "When you feel pure intelligence flowing into you, it may give you sudden strokes of ideas, so that by noticing it, you may find it fulfilled the same day or soon. Those things that were presented unto your minds by the Spirit of God will come to pass, and thus by learning the Spirit of God and understanding it, you may grow into the principle of revelation, until you become perfect in Jesus Christ."[5]

Hearing Him through personal revelation may also come through recalling something we have learned by the Spirit in the past that can apply to the present. The Lord taught this principle in the New Testament: "But the Comforter, which is the Holy Ghost, whom the Father will send in my name, he shall teach you all things, and bring all things to your remembrance, whatsoever I have said unto you" (John 14:26).

We can hear Him as a voice in our mind or as an audible voice.

This happened in the Book of Mormon to Nephi and Lehi, the sons of Helaman. They kept the commandments of God and went forth as missionaries from one city to another, teaching with great power and authority, until they were taken by a Lamanite army and cast into prison. A revelation was given to them and those who had imprisoned them: "They heard [a] voice, and beheld that it was not a voice of thunder, neither was it a voice of great tumultuous noise, but behold, it was a still voice of perfect mildness, as if it had been a whisper, and it did pierce even to the very soul" (Helaman 5:30).

Another example is Enos, who wrestled before God to receive a remission of his sins. He knelt down in prayer, crying out in supplication for his soul, "and there came a voice unto [him], saying Enos, thy sins are forgiven thee, and thou shalt be blessed" (Enos 1:5).

We can hear Him through dreams, visions, and visitations.

Throughout the scriptures, God has communicated with his people through dreams and visions when they needed direction. "Behold, he hath heard my cry by day, and he hath given me knowledge by visions in the night-time" (2 Nephi 4:23). He has also sent messengers from heaven, often in the form of angels, like in the case of Alma: "I have seen an angel face to face, and he spake with me" (Alma 38:7).

Elder Dieter F. Uchtdorf has promised the same for us in our day: "The Everlasting and Almighty God . . . will speak to those who approach Him with a sincere heart and real intent. He will speak to them in dreams, vision, thoughts, and feelings."[6]

Hearing Him can bring us peace.

"These things I have spoken unto you, that in me ye might have peace" (John 16:33). This lets us feel comfort that we are not alone. "If thou shalt ask, thou shalt receive revelation upon revelation, knowledge upon knowledge, that thou mayest know the mysteries and peaceable things—that which bringeth joy" (Doctrine and Covenants 42:61).

He may also respond to our questions when we're trying to make a decision or find out if what we desire is right. "My will . . . shall be signalized unto you by the peace and power of my Spirit, that shall flow unto you" (Doctrine and Covenants 111:8).

We can hear Him through warm feelings.

The Lord teaches how we can recognize if something is right: "But, behold, I say unto you, that you must study it out in your mind; then you must ask me if it is right, and if it is right I will cause that your bosom shall burn within you; therefore, you shall feel that it is right" (Doctrine and Covenants 9:8). Not everyone experiences the Spirit in this way, and the warm feeling—or "burning" as some describe—can vary in intensity.

We can hear Him through feelings of constraint, warning, or confusion.

The definition of *constrain* in the Bible Dictionary is "to be urged strongly to do or not do something, especially by the influence and power of the Holy Ghost" (Bible Dictionary, "Constrain, Constraint"). In the Book of Mormon, after a failed attempt to obtain the brass plates, Nephi said to his brothers, "Let us go up again unto Jerusalem, and let us be faithful in keeping the commandments of the Lord" (1 Nephi 4:1). Reluctantly they followed him to outside the city walls. By night they hid, and Nephi crept toward the house of Laban, being "led by the Spirit, not knowing beforehand the things [he] should do" (1 Nephi 4:6). When he saw a man fallen down drunk, he realized it was Laban. He withdrew Laban's sword, and as he admired its fine workmanship, "it came to pass that [he] was constrained by the Spirit that [he] should kill Laban" (1 Nephi 4:10).

Wilford Woodruff experienced feelings of constraint from the Spirit when he was bringing a group of Saints from New England and Canada to the West. They had scheduled passage on a boat, but the Spirit warned him not to go. He heard a voice say, "Don't go aboard that steamer, nor your company," and he obeyed. The boat departed, and after traveling some fifty yards downstream, it caught fire and sank.[7]

There are times when we ask Heavenly Father if something is right and we hear Him through an impression telling us that what we've asked is not correct. We might feel unsettled or confused. "But if it be not right . . . you shall have a stupor of thought that shall cause you to forget the thing which is wrong" (Doctrine and Covenants 9:9).

We can hear Him when we pray.

"Pray unto the Father with all the energy of heart, that ye may be filled with this love, which he hath bestowed upon all who are true followers of his Son, Jesus Christ . . . that when he shall appear we shall be like Him . . . that we may have hope; that we may be purified even as he is pure" (Moroni 7:48).

Prayer changes things. Prayer brings help, direction, comfort, and answers. Prayer helps us feel God's love for us. It helps us love others, and it also helps us show God that we love Him. Prayers can be offered silently or out loud, anywhere, anytime, and about anything. We should "pray without ceasing" (1 Thessalonians 5:17), knowing that as we "counsel with the Lord in all [our] doings . . . he will direct [us] for good" (Alma 37:37).

We can hear Him when we receive counsel from inspired and directed leaders and others He sends to help us.

President Nelson reassures us, "Ordained Apostles of Jesus Christ always testify of Him. They point the way as we make our way through the heart-wrenching maze of our mortal experiences."[8] The scriptures teach, "He that receiveth the word by the Spirit of truth receiveth it as it is preached by the Spirit of truth. Wherefore, he that preacheth and he that receiveth, understand one another, and both are edified and rejoice together" (Doctrine and Covenants 50:21–22). When truth is taught by the Spirit, the Spirit will testify that the things that have been said are true.

We hear Him when we are led to do something good or to change to become more like Him.

"Put your trust in that Spirit which leadeth to do good—yea, to do justly, to walk humbly, to judge righteously; and this is my Spirit" (Doctrine and Covenants 11:12). Promptings to do good can be from Him. When we feel led to help someone in need, encourage them with our words, or share something we've learned that has helped us; when we treat others with kindness even if they are unkind; when we are prompted to forgive someone or give them grace; or when we give of ourselves, our time, and our means to serve others, then we are acting as He would.

We can hear Him when we attend the temple.

"The house of the Lord is a house of learning. There the Lord teaches in His own way. There each ordinance teaches us about the Savior. There we learn how to rebuke the adversary and draw upon the Lord's priesthood power to strengthen us and those we love. Every minute of time [there] will bless you and your family in ways nothing else can. Take time to ponder what you hear and feel when you are there. Ask the Lord to teach you how to open the heavens and bless your life and the lives of those you love and serve."[9]

We can hear Him when we listen to sacred and uplifting music.

"For my soul delighteth in the song of the heart; yea the song of the righteous is a prayer unto me" (Doctrine and Covenants 25:12). "Praise the Lord with singing [and] with music" (Doctrine and Covenants 136:28). Sacred music can draw us closer to Him by inviting His Spirit. It can have a profound effect on our behavior. It can quiet us, lift us, connect us, combat opposition and negativity, bring us spiritual strength, inspire us, and prepare us for worship.

We can hear Him when we are enjoying the beauty of nature.

When our senses are flooded with His divine artistic and creative power—reflected in majestic mountains, fertile fields, rugged coastlines, and flowing rivers—we can know that "the heavens declare the glory of God; and the firmament sheweth his handywork" (Psalm 19:1). "All things which come of the earth . . . are made . . . both to please the eye and gladden the heart" (Doctrine and Covenants 59:18).

We can hear Him when facing any kind of trial, heartache, loss, or difficult circumstance.

"We all have trials to face—at times very difficult trials. We know the Lord allows us to go through trials in order to be polished and perfected so we can be with Him forever. Our trials and our difficulties give us the opportunity to learn and grow, and they may even change our very nature. If we can turn to the Savior in our extremity, our souls can be polished as we endure."[10]

The Lord taught this to the Prophet Joseph Smith in Liberty Jail: "My son, peace be unto thy soul; thine adversity and thine afflictions shall be but a small moment; and then, if thou endure it well, God shall exalt thee on high; thou shalt triumph over all thy foes" (Doctrine and Covenants 121:7–8).

It's clear that we can hear the Lord in many ways—if only we will listen. The following true stories illustrate this vital truth.

PART I

HEARING HIM THROUGH PRAYER AND SCRIPTURES

"Search diligently, pray always, and be believing, and all things shall work together for your good."

Doctrine and Covenants 90:24

1

"I Love You"

"Pray without ceasing."
1 Thessalonians 5:17

◇◇

One of my fondest memories begins and ends with tears.

At age fifteen, I was dealing with what many other teens do—I hated myself and I craved control. Both of these feelings led, among other things, to a rough relationship with food. It had been a struggle for months, and I was overwhelmed. All I could see was negativity—negativity in the people around me, negativity in things around me, and negativity about myself. It was awful.

One day, I felt a strong urge to kneel down and pray.

Praying was something I hadn't done in a while, at least not the kind of prayer that was sincere and open. This time, when I knelt down to pray to my Heavenly Father, it was different.

I began to thank Him.

I thanked Him for everything.

I thanked Him in spite of everything.

I thanked Him for little things, like trees and sunsets.

I thanked Him for bigger things, like my family and the gospel.

Tears flowed steadily down my face even though my eyes were shut tight.

It wasn't a prayer I would have thought to give until that very moment. I truly had no idea what I was going to say until I spoke. I prayed for several minutes like this, finding anything and everything to be grateful for.

At the end of my prayer, I said, "I love you."

It was so simple.

They were the easiest three words I have ever spoken—and probably the truest. I felt like He didn't hear it enough from me, or from anyone really. I will never forget what happened after I closed my prayer.

I heard, in a voice both strong and soft, "I love you too."

I have never cried so hard in my life as I did in that moment. It took a long time for the tears to stop.

It's been five years since then, but that was the moment that eternally cemented my faith in God. It was such a simple thing to have happened: I said a prayer, and I got a response—immediately.

I didn't just hear it.

I felt everything that was meant with it.

It felt like the warmest memory of my family.

It felt like my favorite song.

It felt like someone had wrapped me in their arms, lifted me up, and took all the weight from off my shoulders.

God knew.

He knew me, He knew what I needed, and He gave me what He could.

"When you know and understand how completely you are loved as a child of God, it changes everything."[2]

It got me out of bed for months. I started a gratitude journal. And even though I have since stopped writing in it, I still remember to tell Him "I love you" and to offer up my gratitude.

Nothing compares to that moment. Nothing in the five years since has even come close. He became my best friend, the person I go to when I need someone to listen, and the person I go to when I see something good happen. I went from barely praying to praying whenever I can. I tell Him about my day or pray to Him on my way to work. Sometimes, when I have a lot of energy to expel, I pray when I run or go for a walk. I pray to say hello, to say thank you, to ask for help, or just because I want to.

He knew. He still knows. His words are engraved on my soul. I've learned to hear Him, and I wouldn't have it any other way.

"As we cheerfully submit our will to the Father, even in the most difficult circumstances, the Savior will lift our burdens and make them light."[1]

Brent H. Nielson

2

HE LAID IT OUT IN MY MIND

"Fear not: peace be unto thee, be strong."
Daniel 10:19

When my husband began to periodically show signs of strange mental behavior, I initially thought it was due to old age—we had been married sixty-two years at that point. As time went on, things grew alarmingly worse. It was extremely difficult when he began to accuse me of being unfaithful to him and our temple covenants, currently and in the past. His unfounded accusations created difficult verbal confrontations that became more frequent and outlandish. Repeatedly I voiced my innocence. At times the interactions turned into shouting matches, which included displays of clenched fists. I continued to defend myself, often growing angry, yet his rantings continued.

Eventually, my children found out about his aggressive behavior. Sadly, during the course of several events, medical appointments, and testing, we realized he truly believed the horrible things he was accusing me of. He was dealing with dementia and verbally abusing me in the process. His erratic behavior occurred at all times of the day and night. My adult daughters that lived nearby often encouraged me to leave the house.

It was a very stressful time.

Through all this, my husband told me that he loved me and wanted me to repent so we could be together in the eternities. It was a great struggle.

In late February 2021, he had been at me all day and night. Finally, at 4 a.m. he got up and left the bedroom, ranting all the way. I remained in bed, pleading in prayer, asking Heavenly Father what course of action I should take.

All of a sudden, a diorama opened before me inside my mind.

The diorama included specific things I needed to do, laid out one by one.

I needed to leave my husband and home—and I was directed where to go.

I was to put new tires on the car first.

I was to bring specific things with me—the majority of my clothes, certain food supplies I had on hand and in my pantry, tax and bill information and receipts, my music, and on and on. I felt impressed to gather things I had never considered needing before, like my sewing machine and supplies.

After I lay there marveling for a while, I got up and began to pack. I didn't cry—I knew I was doing the right thing. I took all the items I had seen in my mind and started packing them into bags and suitcases. Meanwhile, my husband followed me around, yelling the whole time.

I hauled everything to the car and started packing it in. The life I had known with my husband was over. We both began to cry. It was the end of living together as a married couple the way we had for so long, but I *knew* the Lord had told me to go.

Personal revelation, for me, is not a daily thing. However, I ask for it on a daily basis. I have learned in my life that sometimes I hear Him this way—by things being clearly laid out in my mind.

My children are doing their very best to care for us both separately. I have my own apartment, and my husband has home care. I don't know the path that lies ahead, but I know the Lord is with us.

"We need to ask in faith to know the will of the Lord and accept that the Lord knows what is better for us."[1]

Elder Ciro Schmeil

3

WHERE DID I FEEL PEACE?

*"I will instruct thee and teach thee
in the way which thou shalt go."
Psalm 32:8*

I have always been a very stubborn person. Maybe it's because of my red hair, or because I come from a long line of strong-willed people, but more likely it has to do with my fear of not being in control of my own self. In some ways this trait has served me well. For example, I've never had an interest in alcohol, drugs, or anything severely addictive because I have seen how those substances can control people and change their nature or character. In other ways, though, my lack of willingness to be governed by an outside source has made it harder for me to learn how to listen to God.

When I was fourteen, I received my patriarchal blessing. I was young, but I was seeking the Lord, so it was the right time for me. In my blessing, it clearly stated that one day I would serve a full-time mission. I found ways to explain that prophecy away because a mission wasn't something I had in my plans. Like I said—stubborn.

When I became old enough to serve a mission, an impression came to pray about it. I did . . . but not with an open mind. As you might expect, I didn't get an answer. I decided to take that as a "no" and dismissed the idea again.

Several years passed until early in 2020, toward the beginning of the COVID-19 pandemic. I found myself in a low place, lower than ever before.

I had been dating someone for several months, and we had been talking seriously about marriage. Around the same time, things came up in our relationship that caused me a lot of fear regarding a future together. I tried to ignore the fears and doubt, but as an emotionally driven person, this led me to feel increasing anxiety, which was something new for me. I wasn't eating, I cried myself to sleep every night (if I slept at all), and I had to force myself to complete daily tasks. In describing my experience one day in my journal, I wrote, "I have felt a heaviness in my heart and an overall dullness."

I knew I needed to change something, but I was afraid of losing someone I loved. Despite all of this, I kept moving forward, hoping that something would be different so I wouldn't have to face my fear of losing him.

In April 2020, my boyfriend was over at my place with some friends who had come to town. And that's when it hit me. I couldn't keep this up—I was lying to myself and ignoring God. I needed to pray. I needed to truly seek an answer from Him. I told my boyfriend I needed to go to my room for a bit to study and pray. He looked worried but didn't stop me, which I was grateful for.

My bedroom was central in the house and not the most private place, but once inside, I shut the door and turned off my phone. It was still almost impossible to focus with all the outside noise. My head was a mess—I felt sick enough to throw up.

I placed my hands over my ears and started praying, telling God how I felt and pouring out all my fears to Him. One fear I had was whether my boyfriend would be faithful to me—and to God—if we were married. The thought came to ask God about it.

That was the last question I wanted to ask because I was afraid of what the answer would be. But I was in a place where I was willing to do *anything* God told me, as long as it would provide relief from the stress and anxiety that was overwhelming me.

So, I asked *Him*.

The simple answer I received was, "No, he won't."

At first, this shocked me so much that I couldn't even cry. Initially, I wanted to deny the answer and where it had come from—it was the furthest response from what I had wanted to hear. Ultimately, though, I knew.

It felt and sounded like *Him*, through the Holy Ghost. It was a quiet, simple, almost inaudible voice, with no fear attached to it—just gentle knowing. Still, I continued to pray, wanting some other answer to come or an explanation as to why I would still be able to marry him, despite this new knowledge I'd received.

I was led to an old journal of mine. I began reading a passage I'd written about a time when I realized I needed to look to the needs of others more than my own. After reading this, I was given another question to ask the Lord—what does my boyfriend need?

At the time, this question seemed to contradict the last one I had asked, but I was eager to move on, so I asked anyway. The answer came that he needed *me*.

Confusion and frustration were my primary emotions. If he needed me, but was supposedly not going to stay faithful to me, how was I any closer to knowing what I needed to do? I felt like I was backtracking. I started to doubt whether I knew how to hear the Spirit or receive revelation for myself. I explored this thought option for a short time, but after reading parts of my patriarchal blessing and recalling past experiences, I was reminded I'd had too many spiritual witnesses to deny my ability to hear the voice of the Spirit.

After realizing there were no flaws in the answers I had received up to this point, I looked for another way to escape. I considered going out to talk to my boyfriend rather than pushing through my fears and facing God. I wanted to escape into the false security of his arms and hear him tell me everything would be all right.

Knowing this would only give me momentary relief, I continued my wrestle with the Lord.

Covering my ears, I started praying again.

It was a struggle. I felt like I was fighting against myself to get to the Spirit. Finally, I got some direction, but it seemed to make as little sense to me as my previous two questions. I was told to ask my brother to come into my room and that he had an answer for me.

In a short moment, several things went through my head. How would I get my brother to come? I had determined not to leave my room because I knew that once I saw my boyfriend, I would lose all motivation to seek an answer that might take me away from him. And I didn't want to turn my phone back on and have that distraction pull me away from the progress I was making. I also worried that this was me looking for an easy out. If my brother, who I respect and trust, could give me an answer to my struggles, then that would be a lot easier than all the trouble I was going through to get my own answer.

As I was fighting my urge to ignore the prompting, I heard my brother walk past my door. Almost against my own will, I called out and asked him to come into my room.

My sweet brother came without question. Upon shutting the door, I told him what God had told me—that he supposedly had an answer for me. He joked about feeling under pressure, and then he focused and started to ask me questions.

He asked for background on my situation (since he had been out of town for several months) and then started asking more personal questions. Was my boyfriend someone who motivated me to be better?

I couldn't come up with a straightforward answer, so I concluded he didn't. My brother asked why I loved my boyfriend. Once again, I found myself without words. A feeling of hopelessness came over me. Things went on like this for several minutes. My brother would ask me a question, and I would attempt to answer it but with little to no success. At one point, I let out a frustrated laugh and said, in a half-joking manner, "Aren't you supposed to be giving me an answer, not more questions?"

He gently laughed and said simply, "I have one more question. Where do you feel peace?"

As soon as he asked that, I knew it was the answer I had been promised I would receive from him. Again, I had no clear response for him. The two options I had in my mind for my future were to resume life as I had been living—before I'd started dating my boyfriend—or to marry him. The former felt empty, lonely, and lacking in purpose and passion. I knew I would be unhappy; there was no peace in that option. The latter option, to get married despite everything I felt and knew, increased my fear and anxiety—two emotions that are far removed from peace.

My brother smiled at me and said I needed to take this to God now. He was right.

I wrote down the last question he had asked me, gave him a hug, and thanked him. Then he left. I resumed praying, asking God in sincerity,

"Where do I feel peace?" Not long after, I raised my head from a bowed position and looked in front of me even though my prayer wasn't finished.

The Spirit was guiding me.

My eyes rested on my patriarchal blessing, folded in half, lying on my bed. I felt prompted to open to the last page. As I did so, my eyes fell on the one paragraph visible on that half of the page. I reread again my call from the Lord to one day serve a full-time mission.

Tears began to flow as the impression came that *now* was the time for me to serve that mission. It was one of the clearest impressions I'd ever received up to that point in my life.

The idea of serving scared me. What would this mean regarding my future? How would I handle a mission? Would my boyfriend wait for me if I were to go? I let these thoughts take reign for several seconds until I was able to quiet my fears and let this idea breathe. Once I did, every-thing—literally everything—started to make sense.

I thought about the three questions I had been given.

Would my boyfriend be faithful? No. That answer was clear. But if I went on a mission, it would allow time for him to prove himself (or not) without it hurting me as deeply.

What did he need? Me. If I were on a mission, he would have the op-portunity to overcome that dependency and learn to rely wholly on the Lord—or not.

Where did I feel peace?

I paused and said a silent prayer in my heart, asking if serving a mis-sion was really what the Lord wanted me to do right now. In that prayer, I let go of my fears, my hopes, and my desires. I was completely void of any bias. I sincerely wanted to know *His* will. My answer came in the form of peace—overwhelming and beautiful peace! My tears had not ceased to fall during all of this, but now a joyful smile broke through those tears. I tasted a small portion of what the Three Nephites must have felt when they chose to walk a holier path, the path that God had intended for them. Christ said to them, "Your joy shall be full, even as the Father hath given me fulness of joy" (3 Nephi 28:10).

I can say with complete confidence that choosing to serve a full-time mission has been the best decision I have ever made in my life. Not be-cause it was what God wanted me to do, or even because of everything I've learned on my mission so far, but because in that three-hour wrestle with the Lord when I decided to serve a mission, I learned to truly hear

Him. I learned how to humble myself before Almighty God and to submit my foolish, prideful will to His wise and prudent one.

I know that He speaks to us and guides us, exactly how and when we need, if we are willing to be still and hear Him.

"Miracles can come as answers to prayers. They are not always what we ask for or what we expect, but when we trust in the Lord, He will be there, and He will be right."[1]

Ronald A. Rasband

4

A Light unto My Path

*"I am the light of the world: he that followeth
me shall not walk in darkness."*
John 8:12

Repeatedly, when I've been searching for answers to something I'm struggling with, when I'm feeling fear or loneliness, or when I need strength
beyond my own, God has answered me with words from the scriptures.

One of my teenage sons was feeling lost, more than I even realized.
When my understanding of the seriousness of what he was facing became clearer, I faltered under the weight. I was already exhausted from
dealing with other situations going on in our home—a by-product of
having a large blended family—and was aware of the negative effects
these were having on our desired peace and unity. I often felt worn and
overwhelmed, wondering how I would survive this part of my motherhood journey.

One night after a conflict, when I was feeling overcome with heartache, I fell to my knees in desperation to pray. I didn't know how I
could possibly handle another child acting out and feeling broken without losing it myself. During the prayer, I poured my feelings out to my
Heavenly Father, with descriptive details and plenty of tears. After my
pleading prayer ended, a clear impression came to my mind: "You can't

fall apart—even if you feel like it. You are the parent, he is the child, and even though you feel like you're at the point where you've had enough, you need to help him."

The Spirit reminded me that our youth are faced daily with temptations of dozens of kinds, often in ways that harm or hurt their bodies, and being strong and withstanding these temptations is not easy for them. "The adversary works relentlessly to attack the elements of the Father's plans he hates the most. . . . Because he has no physical body, [he] invites and entices us to share in his misery through the improper use of our bodies. The very tool he does not have and cannot use is thus the primary target of his attempt to lure us to physical and spiritual destruction."[2]

This valuable insight humbled me and helped me think about things from my son's perspective. Even though I was emotionally and mentally tired, God softened my heart. It wasn't about "surviving" another teenage son—it was about doing all I could to help *him* survive what he was struggling with.

The situation continued to worsen. I asked my husband to give me a priesthood blessing. I needed to feel God's comfort more deeply through that healing power. Through the words of the inspired blessing, I learned I would be guided further to know exactly how to help my son as I continued to pray and study the scriptures. I was reassured that God would help me stay calm despite what my son said or did that created challenges in our relationship and in our home. I needed to continue "undaunted, trusting in Heavenly Father's care."[3]

Even though my son's pain and the situation weighed heavily on me, I was told, "Let not your heart be troubled, neither let it be afraid" (John 14:27).

I knew God was comforting me through this scripture and that I wasn't alone in this new challenge. He knew me, and He knew my son. This experience reaffirmed to me the importance of studying the scriptures. I needed His help daily in all I did, especially in my role as a parent. When I made reading and studying the scriptures a priority, even if it was just for a few minutes each day, I was more in tune to hear Him. The scriptures, or God's word, "is a lamp unto my feet, and a light unto my path" (Psalm 119:105).

Four months later, my son attempted suicide.

The night it happened, I knew darkness was in our home. Not realizing the gravity of the situation, but feeling intense desperation for heavenly intervention, I petitioned God in prayer more powerfully than I ever had in my life. I cried out to the Father, begging Him to send help. After my knees grew sore, I crawled into bed and attempted to sleep. Rest came fitfully at best.

Early the next morning, a Sunday, I awoke feeling an urge to go to my son's bedroom and give him a hug. When I entered, he was still asleep. I walked across the room and gently touched him on the shoulder. He stirred groggily and then sat up, seeming a little confused. I leaned in to hug him, and he clung to me for a few minutes. I don't recall him ever hanging on to me before in that way. I had no idea at the time that he hadn't expected to wake up that morning still alive.

Later we learned from another priesthood blessing that our son had been surrounded by ministering angels that night, and one in particular was working very hard to help him. God had heard my prayer. *He* had sent help. "I will be with thee: I will not fail thee, nor forsake thee. Be strong and of a good courage" (Joshua 1:5–6).

"As we come unto Him, God will come to our rescue, whether to heal us or to give us the strength to face any situation."[1]

Walter F. Gonzalez

5

In the Valleys of Our Lives

"He will guide you into all truth . . .
and he will shew you things to come."
John 16:13

My husband started receiving strong spiritual direction that we needed to sell our home and move out of state. We had lived in our current home less than a year and were just beginning to feel settled in the area and in the ward. When he shared with me what he had been feeling, I was not happy. I didn't want to move for many reasons, including the fact I felt I was still adjusting to other recent and difficult changes in my life. How could the Lord expect me to handle another big transition such as this?

Thinking about what it would entail—like quitting a job I loved, being far away from several of my adult children, and leaving close friends to live in an area of the country I was completely unfamiliar with where I knew absolutely no one—caused me to be overcome with fear. I knew the fear was not of God, "for God hath not given us the spirit of fear; but of power, and of love, and of a sound mind," (2 Timothy 1:7). But moving at that time in my life felt like too huge of a hurdle to cross.

I knew I couldn't face all it would involve, or even be able to move forward to begin, unless I felt certain it was Heavenly Father's will. I prayed and fasted to receive the same confirmation my husband had received, and I cried a lot. I knew I could trust the Lord in everything, but this was so not what I wanted, nor was it anything I had expected to be asked to do. God hadn't said why He wanted us to move—just that we were supposed to.

My husband gave me a priesthood blessing, which brought some clarity and comfort, but still I struggled. When Sunday came, we attended church together in our ward. As I looked around and saw many faces that had grown dear to me, I felt more sadness about leaving. During the sacrament ordinance, I prayed again to receive an answer—to know if moving was God's will for us. Then, a scripture filled my mind: "For I will go before your face. I will be on your right hand and on your left, and my Spirit shall be in your hearts, and mine angels round about you to bear you up" (Doctrine and Covenants 84:88).

I knew that verse had come from God. It was His way of telling me He was with me and that I didn't need to fear. Still, a part of me resisted. *But this isn't what I want, Lord!*

God taught me further by reminding me of the words in a song from the *Children's Songbook* about Nephi: "I will go; I will do the thing the Lord commands. I know the Lord provides a way; he wants me to obey."[2]

Those words humbled me. Tears filled my eyes. I was grateful He answered, even if it was different than I had expected.

I love President Nelson's counsel when he tells us that the first word in the Doctrine and Covenants is to *hearken*. In the Old Testament, we learn that the Hebrew word *shema* is a verb that means "to listen with the intent to obey." When we hear Him, or *hearken,* we are following a pattern for success, happiness, and joy in our lives. President Nelson says, "We are to *hear* the words of the Lord, *hearken* to them, and *heed* what He has told us!"[3]

Over the next few weeks, I vacillated between knowing this was something I could do to wanting to say it felt too hard. I had *heard* Him, and I wanted to *heed* Him, but I was struggling. So many changes had to occur to facilitate such a big transition in our lives, and we didn't know how it would all come together. We felt at times that we were walking into the darkness because there were so many unknowns. We knew we needed to trust God, especially since He was in charge, but at the same time we had a lot of things to figure out. We continued to be prayerful.

Elder Scott gave this counsel: "When we seek inspiration to help make decisions, the Lord gives us gentle promptings. These require us to think, to exercise faith, to work, to struggle at times, and to act. Seldom does the whole answer to a decisively important matter or complex problem come all at once. More often, it comes a piece at a time, without the end in sight."[4]

Together, my husband and I decided we needed to take a trip to the state where we felt we were supposed to move to. We thought, "Maybe the move will actually be sometime in the future—not something imminent," and a part of me hoped that was the answer. Meanwhile, the next logical step seemed for us to go, check out the general area my husband had received promptings about, and see how we felt actually being there. We knew that if this was the Lord's will, He would continue to guide us.

Two days later we were on our way. It was a sixteen-hour drive. We stopped the first night at a hotel and then continued the next morning, totally going on faith. Late the second day, we pulled into a large city under a torrential rainstorm. The dark sky, ribboned with thunder and lightning, felt cold and unwelcoming, as did the maze of unfamiliar freeways. We were tired, overwhelmed by uncertainty, and struggling with doubts about why we were there.

After checking into the hotel, we prayed for continued help and guidance. We knew we had to keep pushing forward with faith, knowing that if it was God's will for us to move—which we believed it was—then He would show us how, even when we felt the doubts surface. Just like Alma teaches, exercising faith is a process. "If ye will awake and arouse your faculties, even to an experiment upon my words, and exercise a particle of faith, yea, even if ye can no more than desire to believe, let this desire work in you, even until ye believe in a manner that ye can give place for a portion of my words" (Alma 32:27).

The next morning, we began with hope—hope that God was with us, that we would continue to hear Him, and that His plan would unfold. We looked at many homes and properties that day. One in particular we came across by chance after we saw a "For Sale" sign in one of the areas we liked. When we pulled into the driveway to get a closer look, we saw a woman sitting under a large, shady oak tree. She walked toward us as we got out of the car. We found out she was a realtor waiting for a client who wanted to tour the home. She gave us her card and let us look at the house as well. We liked it, and we liked the area, but it didn't necessarily feel "right." Nothing else we looked at that day did either.

The next day was Sunday, and we wanted to go to church. We searched the internet to find the closest Latter-day Saint meetinghouse location and got ready to go. My husband was battling with feelings of discouragement over not knowing what to do. We were both tired from spending several days in the car, driving from one unfamiliar area to the next hoping we would stumble on the place God wanted us to be. We needed to head home in two more days so we could get back to work and our other commitments. We had been praying repeatedly for direction and guidance, but nothing felt clear.

During the sacrament, I prayed silently for help and direction. The thought came to contact the realtor we had met yesterday. After church, I shared with my husband what I had felt. Thankfully, he had saved the realtor's card in his wallet. I sent her a brief text telling her who I was and asking if she could help us. She responded within five minutes. A short time later we talked together on the phone. We told her what we were looking for in general, and she said she would be glad to help by sending some listings. Later that night she sent over several.

My husband was taking care of some paperwork when I opened the text the realtor sent and started reviewing the listings online. When I came to the fourth listing and clicked on it, I *felt* something. With each picture I viewed, followed by a detailed description of the property, the feeling grew stronger. Something was drawing me to that house. I got my husband's attention and told him he needed to look at it. He wasn't as excited as I was initially, but he did agree it had possibilities. When we looked through the rest of the listings, two others caught our attention but not as strongly as the first one had.

I texted the realtor and told her we would like to see three of the listings. She confirmed about an hour later with our appointment times for the following morning. The house I was drawn to the most was first on the schedule.

The next morning, we reviewed the map and planned out what time we would need to leave to make our appointment. As we did so, we discovered that the first house was in the exact city and county my husband had felt directed by the Lord to move to. That got the attention of both of us. Our excitement increased the closer we got to the house. With all the rain the area had received over the past several days, the open yard was lush and green. When I got out of the car to gaze over the view, I was struck by how peaceful the area was. We spent an hour walking through the house, taking it all in.

Afterward we looked at the other two listings. Neither of them felt right. We thanked our realtor and told her we would get back to her after lunch. My husband and I talked together, shared what we had felt about the first house, and then prayed. We both got the same answer. We called the realtor back and made an offer on the first house. We were nervous but at peace. We trusted that if it was right, it would all work out.

That evening we heard back from the realtor—our offer had been accepted! She was very surprised at how smoothly it had gone, especially since the market was crazy and most sellers were holding out for multiple offers to drive the selling price up. She also told us the sellers hadn't been planning on listing the house until the following weekend because of the rain, but they had decided last minute to list it anyway. We knew if they had waited, we wouldn't have gotten that house because we would have returned home by then.

God had been guiding us. He helped us find exactly the place where He wanted us to be.

We drove home and got our house on the market by the end of that week. Three days later we had multiple offers. As we prepared to move, and then did move, I felt reassured many times that it was *His* will. None of it felt easy, but we were directed and led through all the details, and we were blessed. I was reminded again how grateful I am God is in charge. He doesn't stand on a mountaintop looking down—He is at work with us, His creation, in the valleys of our lives, unfolding His plan and giving comfort and guidance. He promises, "I will never leave thee, nor forsake thee" (Hebrews 13:5).

*"The Lord never asks the impossible.
Often the difficult, but never
the impossible."*[1]

David B. Haight

6

ANSWERED PRAYERS—LGBTQ+

"Pray in your families unto the Father, always in my name, that . . . your children may be blessed."
3 Nephi 18:21

◇◇

I had no how idea many children in conservative family environments try to stifle their true selves, hide emotions, overachieve, and be very careful how they act so as not to let anyone see their true selves . . . until it became personal for me.

Years ago, my adult married son came to me in private, telling me he felt he was actually a female. He hurt so intensely that he was considering suicide because *she* could no longer live this way.

My child had never been in trouble in school and had been an overachiever in education, sports, and leadership callings. He had faithfully served a two-year mission for The Church of Jesus Christ of Latter-day Saints, was married in the temple to a kind and beautiful woman, and was one of the strongest men I knew.

I was overcome with disbelief and shock, having no clue this was how she felt. My heart pounded and my mind swirled as if everything was suddenly torn from beneath my feet, yet I knew falling apart wasn't an option. My child needed me—and I needed God.

I prayed.

"Please, Lord, don't let me mess this up. I have no idea what to say, and if I say the wrong thing, I am so afraid I will lose my precious child!"

I had no other words.

It was seconds, mere seconds, but it was the third time in my adult life that seconds counted more than ever.

The first time was in the hospital with an eleven-year-old son who had been perfectly healthy until suddenly he was paralyzed. An unheard-of diagnosis ended up changing my child's life—and therefore mine—forever.

The second time was a phone call I received at 8 p.m. on an otherwise normal evening, informing me that our twelve-year-old son, the youngest of six, had been hit by a car and was being life-flighted. Twelve days later he graduated from this mortal life.

Once more, my heart and mind were thrust into a life-changing event in which I felt totally unprepared.

My soul immediately longed for the right words to *fix* my child and *fix* the situation. I loved her more than I could express. I wanted to throw my arms around her, protect her from the world, and let my hugs and kisses make her feel better, just as they used to when she was a young child. But I felt clueless about how to respond.

I was scared.

If I said the wrong thing, I was terrified I might damage this precious relationship or unintentionally cause further hurt and pain, especially with my reputation of speaking unfiltered. I longed to know how to ask angels from heaven to bring me a glowing tablet with the perfect answers written on it about how to face this. Instead, I smiled and said, "Hey, the good news is I hear everyone in heaven gets to wear a dress!"

Tears welled in her eyes as she looked at me slightly confused; then we laughed and reached toward each other to embrace.

In my imperfectness, I had spoken from desperation as a lost mother having a real moment. Once my heart calmed, I simply said, "I love you. There is nothing you can do or say that will change how I feel for you. We are going to walk this path and figure it out together."

I've realized that my feelings of being unprepared for another moment like this were wrong. In truth, I had been preparing for years. I had sought to understand the nature of my Heavenly Father, practiced prayer, and read and studied the scriptures since I was a child. I had also worked at developing a close relationship with my Savior, intentionally trying to walk with Him—*hear Him*—throughout my life.

Once I switched my heart and mind to "receiving the Spirit" mode, I was able to respond in a way that helped my child feel loved and safe. The Holy Ghost strengthened me. It was an authentic and imperfect moment, but in my voice my daughter heard reassurance, love, and faith that we were going to be okay. I was willing to walk with her even though I clearly didn't know what I was doing.

With the Savior, I had been preparing for years to trust Him to help me handle things I could not carry by myself. He knows us from the beginning and where we are currently. He has the power to heal and guide us. I was not alone in this. The Savior was beside me.

While I held my child in my arms, the words of a favorite scripture comforted me: "Likewise the Spirit also helpeth our infirmities: for we know not what we should pray for as we ought: but the Spirit itself maketh intercession for us with groanings which cannot be uttered" (Romans 8:26).

If anyone was infirm at that moment, I was. If anyone had no words but inner groanings and pleadings, I did.

Hard experiences in life have driven me to my knees in prayer. At times, I have been utterly devastated and frustrated when I felt my prayers were not being answered, or when they were not the answers I wanted. I wondered what had I done that would make Him give me the silent treatment. Could I have greater faith? Could I be a better person? What was expected of me so I could get Him to talk to me? And if He could send an angel that could talk or write notes for me, that would be really helpful!

When I feel sorry for myself and dramatically try to picture myself as a tree blowing alone in the storm, I immediately feel Him roll His eyes and hug me. Then impressions enter my heart: "Be patient—the answer is coming, but it may take a while" or "The situation isn't yet opened up. You are not yet prepared for the answer. More knowledge is needed." Read more, make a decision, take action, trust the still small voice in your soul, and know as it says in the scriptures, "All things work together for good to them that love God, to them who are called according to his purpose" (Romans 8:28).

My mortal expectation of prayer is similar to everyone else's: answers should be immediate. I should feel or hear them clearly with a warm burning like what is mentioned in the scriptures.

But in a humble home, inside a quiet room, with my frightened and hurting child, surrounded by unfolded laundry on the bed and dirty dishes in the nearby kitchen, our loving Savior reached into my heart and taught me the power of praying, even when it's done imperfectly.

He does not need to send angels to send answers.

If I continue to connect to Him through prayer, I can trust Him completely. I grow in strength from each prayer and experience, learning to more quickly and easily recognize the Spirit and His guidance. There are no shortcuts. We all have spiritual growth to do. It's a lifelong process to become the true disciples and glorious beings He believes we can be, and our prayers are heard *every time.*

In this difficult thing I experienced with my child, I *needed* answers—not just wanted them. I was sure the right answer would *fix* the situation and make it all better, but hearing Him taught me something different. I learned my child does not need me to fix her because she is not broken. Her feelings are real even though I didn't understand how or why.

Another lesson followed with the same firmness and tone that entered my soul when my younger son lay in a hospital bed taking his last breath years before. The other eight children in the pediatric intensive care unit that day were going to heal, but not *my* son. I learned I would find nothing in asking God why or by comparing. Questioning *why* would not have raised my younger son from his hospital bed. And now, years later, questioning *why* would not change how my older child, who identifies as female, thinks or feels inside or sees the world. What *could* change things, and the only change I had control over, was listening to the Savior to know who I was and what I could do.

I needed to concentrate my prayers on *how.*

Now I pray for things like how I can be a better mother, how I can be a better wife, how I can help my neighbors, how I can be a better disciple, and how I can love my Savior more fully and deeply.

When I pray for *how,* I live more intentionally. I can better use my talents, time, and resources to help others. I can pray to more clearly recognize promptings and be more willing to bend my will to His. I am strengthened when I pray for *how* instead of *why.*

My daughter has since left the Church after that day she came to me suffering and in pain. And after a loving and challenging year of counseling and soul searching, she and her spouse divorced but remain close friends.

Why do I write of prayer if things didn't turn out the way I planned or envisioned for my children since the day they were born? Here are my imperfect discoveries:

Not everything will be healed on earth.

Not every answer will be positive.

Not every problem will be solved.

I pray for inclusion for my daughter every day and clarity in our religious environment that will provide safety, peace, and happiness for all the children of God. Prayer has helped lighten my spirit and given me joy with my family members so immeasurable that I struggle to explain it. I cannot be the mother my daughter needs without prayer and connection to the Savior.

I have felt God's love for my daughter. I see His hand in her life and am truly happy for all her accomplishments and the life she has built. We may not agree at the moment in all things spiritual, but we agree life gets better and better, and our relationship with one another is fuller and more loving than ever.

Through hearing Him, I am able to leave my worries at *His* feet, finding the tools that help me build a more beautiful life. He has blessed my efforts. He has provided tender mercies and miracles, lovingly inspiring me about how to better fulfill my purpose. My direction is clearer, and my ability to love and embrace others is greater and still improving.

He has helped remove my self-importance, showing me that my choices and station in life make me no better or greater than anyone else. He helps me remove judgment, replacing it with a heart that desires to serve and learn from others. Through prayer, I have filled my heart with more gratitude. Prayer is my lifeline, my everything. It is the source of communication beyond anything else in the world that allows me to hear Him—feel Him—in all things in my life.

"As you use your agency to carve out time every day to draw close to God's voice, especially in the Book of Mormon, over time His voice will become clearer and more familiar to you."[1]

Michelle Craig

7

HE ANSWERED IMMEDIATELY

"Love one another; as I have loved you."
John 13:34

One Sunday, I attended church with my husband. When we entered the building, an incident occurred in which another member of the ward acted unkindly towards me. This caused me feelings of rejection, and I took it further by questioning why I was even attending that day. I had come hoping to feel rest from the challenges of the week and to feel renewed, but instead I felt hurt.

We took our seats in the chapel, and the negative feelings I was having towards that member continued to plague me. I struggled through the opening hymn and prayer, fighting little seeds of irritation and surprised by how quickly my thoughts had tumbled to a lower place. I knew if I continued to dwell on them, they could prevent me from feeling the Spirit, and I knew I needed strength that day—the strength that hearing Him always brought me.

While the sacrament was being prepared, I prayed to my Heavenly Father. I quickly told Him in my mind what I was feeling and why.

He answered me immediately.

He reminded me that I could choose joy regardless of what happened to me. He also counseled me to give the person who had hurt me grace, just as He gives *me* grace when I make mistakes.

"The people around us are not perfect. People do things that annoy, disappoint, and anger. In this mortal life it will always be that way. Nevertheless, we must let go of our grievances, Part of the purpose of mortality is to learn how to let go of such things. That is the Lord's way."[2]

His reassurance that I was loved by *Him* filled my heart, and the negative feelings I experienced were swept away, replaced with understanding and feelings of good will towards the other member. I realized I could have even misjudged the other person's actions. I felt a renewed sense of comfort and gratitude for the quick lesson—an important reminder to "be ye kind to one another, tenderhearted, forgiving one another, even as God for Christ's sake hath forgiven you" (Ephesians 4:32).

"The more we allow the love of God to govern our minds and emotions—the more we allow our love for our Heavenly Father to swell within our hearts—the easier it is to love others with the pure love of Christ."[3]

PART II

Hearing Him through the Holy Ghost

"Most frequently, revelation comes in small increments over time and is granted according to our desire, worthiness, and preparation."[1]

David A. Bednar

8

The Power of Listening

"Therefore, if you will ask of me you shall receive."
Doctrine and Covenants 6:5

I am still trying to figure out what it looks like, feels like, and sounds like to truly hear the Savior, but I think it's about building an intimate relationship with Him. It's about blocking out and tuning in. It's about humility and love in their purest forms. It's about trust. And the beauty of it is that it's personal. The way Jesus enters my story and speaks to me, fills my empty places, forgives me, and lifts me—and everything else He so willingly does for me—is individual. I always have a means to hear Him. I have access to His guidance, protection, peace, and power in my life. I just have to listen.

So simple, right? Then why is it so hard sometimes?

For me, it takes practice. And patience. And desire. And then more practice. The Lord has blessed me with opportunities to step up, to listen, to hear His voice, and to act, even when it has taken great courage. This has been especially true in my role as a mother of five children.

I love my children with all my heart. I see their goodness! I see their struggles. I want to help them fulfill their divine destinies as children of the Almighty God. But I cannot do this alone. Developing a relationship with Christ, where He talks and I listen, has become vitally important.

It's not easy. I know I miss things. I'm not perfect at it. It involves practice and patience and failure. But it is so worth it!

Eleven years ago, our lives changed forever when the Lord gave us unexpected direction concerning our family. Although we felt blessed to have four children, suddenly it felt like someone was missing. And then those small but significant nudges began. You know the ones—those little moments of spiritual enlightenment that make you start to think that God has something unimaginable in store for you. I love those nudges! But they are not for the weary. I've learned to buckle up when I notice them because surely they will require great amounts of faith and sacrifice.

We started to pray for direction, and our suspicions were confirmed—we needed to bring another child into our home. We immediately started to prepare for another pregnancy. But as we took measures to start down this familiar path, it simply did not feel right. A few months went by, and my husband and I both began to feel that this was not a good idea. We started to consider that the Lord had different plans for us.

As I look back now, I realize the miracle of it all—how He gave inspiration and revelation in small doses all along the journey as we took steps forward. I learned that *listening* is an active word. It means constantly yielding our hearts to Him, allowing Him to direct each vital step, trusting in His timetable, and remembering His wisdom and power to work miracles in our lives.

I still wonder how different our lives would be had we ignored those quiet, almost imperceptible nudges that made us feel we needed to pay attention and seek the Lord for more direction. It started with the tiniest light, the smallest glimpse that there was more for us. It would have been easy to miss or ignore. But as we allowed our hearts to follow those small but significant bursts of light, little by little they became a beam, and we were blessed with the personal revelation we so desperately needed.

I remember clearly the moment I mentioned the word *adoption* to my husband. We were driving in the car. We were discussing our situation, and we felt confused. Why would the Lord lead us to think we needed to bring another child into the world, but then give us the distinct impression to not get pregnant? What was He trying to tell us? Suddenly the words spilled out: "Maybe we're supposed to adopt."

And there it was.

Once we started really opening our minds and hearts to this idea, it became obvious this is what the Lord had been leading us to discover. It felt right. It even began to fill us with excitement. Little did we know we were beginning a journey that would test and try us in ways we could not imagine.

We began to consider our options. The thought of adopting a baby began to nearly consume me. I knew this was our answer, and I was determined to move forward full throttle. Yet as we dove headfirst into the reality of what it would cost monetarily, discouragement settled in. It wasn't realistic to think we could pull this off. Now what?

It would have been easy to give up, to just throw our arms in the air and say it was impossible, to quit before we had really even begun. After all, every means we tried to invent to create resources to move forward only revealed obstacles. But here's the thing—I knew quite a bit about Jesus. I had felt His power in my life before at times when things seemed impossible. I knew He knew the way for us to accomplish the daunting task before us. In fact, I knew He *was* the way! He softened the king's heart when Esther approached him in an effort to save her people. He raised a dying child from the depths of illness, despite the laughter and mocking insults of those outside. He helped Nephi obtain the brass plates and build a boat. If He did that for them, He can do this for me.

Following promptings from the Lord does not mean there won't be obstacles along the way. When Jesus invites me to "be not faithless; only believe" (Mark 5:36), I have to understand that *believe* is a powerful word! It means more than a faint desire. It means taking my eyes off the hurdles in front of me, blocking out the noise from the world, and focusing completely on Him. It means seeking the light for the next step along the process. It means remembering that He will fill in all the missing pieces, connect all the straying dots, and simply provide.

I felt this transformation take hold in my heart. I felt the Spirit whisper to me that things would work out. I felt the Savior beckon to me to simply trust. And so I did. My husband was more hesitant. He is an accountant by trade, and the numbers simply didn't add up. At times he wanted to close the door on the idea, but I knew—I *knew*—that God would provide the ram in the thicket if we would just take that trek up the mountainside. I had no idea how the miracle would be provided—I just knew it would be. After all, Nephi also taught us that God does not command something without providing a way, right?

I started researching adoption agencies. I made phone calls. I wrote lists. I prayed for guidance. I did it without my husband because he wasn't ready to commit quite yet. I found an adoption agency that felt right, and I began filling out all the paperwork, doing all the necessary things so we would be ready at any moment. It was not easy. But I felt I was on the right track, so I kept going. The hardest part was finding unity with my husband about it all. I was so determined to move forward and trust the Lord, but he was struggling to take the dive off that cliff. Sometimes the strain on our marriage felt heavy, and I wondered how to navigate it all. I knew this adoption was important to our family, but I couldn't allow it to sever my relationship with my husband, and it was difficult to balance it all.

Finally, after a few months, my husband was ready. I felt so much gratitude for his willingness to put aside his fears and doubts so we could move forward. The very thing that for months had driven us apart was now the thing that would unite us in valuable ways.

We finished the final steps in the process, submitted the paperwork, and waited. Every day I hoped for the phone to ring to tell us we were being considered for a baby. Before long, we got a very unexpected call one morning from the agency. They asked if we would be willing to consider two babies instead of just one. They shared with us the circumstance of a mother across the country who had called and felt a desperate need to place her two baby girls—a seventeen-month-old and a three-year-old— for adoption. We only had a few short hours to get back to them with an answer.

We were a bit overwhelmed by the call. We had never thought of two babies at once! We didn't have time to fast about it or go to the temple to pray and receive the power and revelation that come from that holy place. We could only pray and listen for anything that might tell us this was not the right decision. We felt no warning or hint that we shouldn't move forward, so we did.

We immediately bought plane tickets for the mother and her two young babies. We spent the week preparing and buying clothing, diapers, and everything we thought we might need. We set up the bedroom for two, and with each act of preparation, we felt the excitement grow within us. We had never met these babies, but somehow we loved them! We felt extraordinarily blessed that our family would welcome two new children instead of just one. We couldn't wait for their arrival!

Unfortunately, it never happened.

We were devastated.

The night before the anticipated day, the birth mom confirmed she would fly out the next morning, and then she was never heard of again. The agency tried over and over to contact her but to no avail. My husband and I worried for her safety and the safety of her precious babies. We prayed and prayed that she would reach out again, but she never did.

Our hearts were broken. I mourned for babies I had never even met or held. I spent hours in my closet, gut-wrenching sobs pouring from my soul. I felt defeated. My soul ached. And I struggled to understand the reasons why everything seemed to be falling apart.

At this point, my desire to become a mother again filled every corner of my heart, and I yearned for the reassurance and peace only the Savior could give. The agency had told us it was possible but very rare for an adoption to fall through. In all of their years of working with mothers and families, they had only had one mother back out. And yet here we were, stumbling to recover from a failed adoption. The hardest part might have been the heartbreak of our other four children. We were on a roller coaster ride that included all of us, and I felt terrible for the heaviness and sadness our children were feeling.

We didn't have much time to mourn because the agency called again just days later. There was another mother. She was due in four months with a baby girl, and they felt we were the best match. Although this may be hard to understand, it was difficult to say yes. We felt a bit broken and bruised, and we weren't sure we were ready to put our hearts on the line again. We were even more hesitant because we'd have to wait several months for the baby to be born before we'd know if the mother would actually follow through. What should we do? What if this happened again? We didn't have answers to these questions, and we felt uncertainty creep in. I did the only thing I could think of to do—I went to the Lord.

As I prayed for faith and understanding, I felt the impression to let go of the previous adoption experience and remember that those babies were in the Lord's care. For whatever reason, we were not the parents who would raise them. I realized the Savior was beckoning me to trust *Him*. I had to give up the control I was desperately clinging to and allow Him to do His work.

As I gave in and strived to really listen, I was suddenly reminded of something a social worker from the adoption agency had told us when she came for a home evaluation. She said, "I've been doing this for a lot of years, and I can tell you that the right children end up in the right homes somehow." These words reminded me that I could yield my heart to the Lord without reservation and trust the process that would bring the right baby to our home. I felt the Spirit reassure me that this adoption we were about to commit to had a bigger purpose than I had originally considered. This was more than the excitement of a new baby joining our home; this was something of an eternal nature, and the Lord was directing each step. We moved forward, and finally the day of the baby's arrival came.

We had to wait a couple of extra days to visit due to the birth mom's wishes, but I will never forget the day we first went to the hospital to see and hold and love this anticipated baby. She was somehow familiar to me. I knew she was ours from the very first moment I saw her and held her close to me, and I loved her immediately and deeply. I understood then that the social worker was exactly right. These miraculous babies find their way to the right homes, and with the Lord's help, she had found ours. I suddenly understood how the timing of it all had been carefully orchestrated by the Lord and how each hurdle we faced had led us to this perfect moment. We would never be the same! The adoption papers were signed and we had our missing piece.

However, this story doesn't end there because now we had to figure out how to pay the large debt we incurred during the process.

This time, the communication from heaven was direct and clear. It was in the earliest hours of morning when the family was still sleeping. I was feeding our sweet baby when suddenly an idea came to my mind that was not my own. Immediately I knew exactly what to do. After weeks of sincere prayer and useless ideas, we had a solution. We got to work and built a wall that separated the main living area and the basement, fasted and prayed for a family to rent our main floor, and moved downstairs.

This arrangement made it possible for us to completely pay for the adoption debt within one year. God had provided the way, and it was miraculous to us! It required sacrifice and determination, but it brought unique blessings too. After all, we learned to wash dishes without a dishwasher, to manage with only one bathroom between the seven of us, and to enjoy a lot of family togetherness as we lived in a cramped space! It was a unique and grand experience for our family to sacrifice in that way.

Throughout this adoption process, I had a glimpse of the Savior's grace, mercy, generosity, and love, and it was completely and wonderfully overwhelming. The Lord generously helped me hear Him in new and profound ways! I will never forget it.

I have found that sometimes answers come immediately; some come after months and months of pondering and searching; some come unexpectedly; some come with certainty; and some come with a need to move forward with faith, hoping I'm getting it right. But they do come. It's impossible to describe every instance when I have heard the Lord speak to me about my role as a mother. Impressions come as I strive to listen. I'm not perfect at hearing His voice, but I am learning how often He is willing to speak to me and give me those vital nudges that end up making all the difference.

Impressions and personal inspiration come often in regards to my family and others: love harder, embrace longer, find something good to say, just listen, send a text of encouragement, leave a note on a mirror or bed, spend some one-on-one time with this child, don't sweat the small stuff, use the scriptures to teach. These promptings, and many more, remind me that Christ is in the trenches with me. He is there to help me as I strive to lead my children on their journey back home.

God is real and He knows us. He invites us to live an abundant life. I hope I never get so busy that I don't take time to listen. I hope I don't allow the clutter and noise of the world and its demands to drown out the voice of the One who loves me most and can give me all I need. I hope I never stop seeking answers. I hope I will live so that His love will resonate in my soul always and provide me with the much-needed guidance I seek. I hope that no matter what else happens in my life, I will always make sure to do all I can to hear Him.

"*Learn of me, and listen to my words;
walk in the meekness of my Spirit, and
you shall have peace in me.*"

Doctrine and Covenants 19:23

9

MISSING CELESTIAL GLORIES

"And be not conformed to this world; but be ye
transformed by the renewing of your mind."
Romans 12:2

◇◇◇

When I was nineteen, I turned in my mission papers and waited with
great anticipation to find out where I would be called to serve. I was hoping to go somewhere foreign where I would be able to learn a language.
Someone in my ward sent in their mission papers around the same time,
and he got his mission call weeks before I did—to Helena, Montana. I
grew more and more eager waiting for my call.

When it finally came, I had to wait even longer to get everyone over
to open it. Finally, I was thrilled to find out I was going to Tonga and
would be learning the Tongan language. I would be entering the Provo
Mission Training Center (MTC) a few months later.

I was with the first group of missionaries who served after the an-
nouncement that young men could serve at age eighteen and young
women at age nineteen. After this change, missionaries going to Tonga
went from a nine-week language program to a six-week language program at the MTC. During the accelerated program, I felt I was progressing decently with the language. My pronunciation definitely had an
American accent, but I felt I could talk and at least bear my testimony. I

grew more and more eager to leave as we neared the end of our time in the MTC. I wanted to get out and serve the people in the Kingdom of Tonga and could not wait to get started.

We left in March when there was still snow on the ground in Utah. After a whole day of flying and layovers, we landed in Nuku'alofa, Tonga. It was the middle of summer there, and it was *hot*. Once we got out of the plane and onto the tarmac, I sweated through my white button-up shirt in five minutes.

I met my trainer and then headed to the area where we were assigned. The area covered three small towns called Hakame, Ha'alalo, and 'Utulau. We lived in Hakame and walked to the rest of the areas whenever we needed to go.

Once I got to Hakame, I realized I was not as prepared as I thought. I was surrounded by people that spoke fluently and at a much faster pace than what I had encountered in the MTC. I felt like Elder Calhoun in the film *The Best Two Years*. When he gets to Holland, he asks what language the native people were speaking, and when his companion says, "Dutch," Elder Calhoun replies, "That's not what they taught me in the MTC!"

I felt I was in over my head and could not understand anything that was going on. I love to talk, and not being able to do so was absolute torture. I would go to an appointment and the only way I was able to participate was to either bear my testimony or say a sentence in extremely broken Tongan. I felt like a failure. I felt like I was letting the Lord down. I hated that my companion had to pull all the weight and that I was not able to support him. It was depressing. I wondered how I was going to get through the next two years.

A month into serving in Tonga, my companion and I were on our way home from 'Utulau. It had been an extremely long day. As all meals were provided by members, we were dependent upon the wards to feed us, and that day, the person responsible had forgotten to get us dinner. We had spent all day teaching, and I felt I had understood less that day than any day previous. I was discouraged and feeling down. I was hungry. I was tired.

The road from 'Utulau was not lit, and it was a moonless night as my companion and I walked the twenty-five-minute journey home. I tried to focus on the road so I wouldn't trip and hurt my feet—especially since we wore flip flops with our traditional Tongan skirts instead of the typical lace-up shoes and dress pants. It was impossible to see the path, but I was still trying to peer through the darkness, hoping to perceive and avoid the bumps, dips, and rocks in my path.

While I was looking down, my companion, whose eyes were lifted, noticed three or four shooting stars in the sky above. I love astronomy, and shooting stars are among my favorite things to see. I felt even more depressed that I had missed them and was not in a good place mentally.

At this low point, I received a distinct impression: *I will miss the celestial glories around me if I focus on the things I cannot change.*

I had been focusing on the hard things immediately in front of me with a downward gaze instead of looking up toward God. This prompting gave me a completely different perspective during the rest of my mission. I started focusing on what I could control. I started reminding myself I was not perfect and would not be able to learn a new language in a matter of weeks. I started focusing on my language studies and worked on participating more in the lessons. I started seeing the beauty in that journey.

Eventually, I got over my fear and started trusting the Lord to bless me in learning the language. After about three and a half months, I felt like I could hold my own in any conversation.

I know the Lord blesses those who diligently put in effort over time and that He will help us achieve worthy goals. I know the Lord is aware of me and will bless me when I work hard on improving and turning to Him.

"Wherefore, I said unto you, feast upon the words of Christ; for behold, the words of Christ will tell you all things what ye should do."

2 Nephi 32:3

10

WHISPERINGS OF THE SPIRIT

"Let the Holy Spirit guide;
Let him teach us what is true."[1]

In the heat of the COVID-19 pandemic of 2020, I was attending school online through BYU–Idaho. One day I was sitting in our kitchen doing homework when my husband walked into our house. This was unusual because it was during our daughters' nap time, and he never came home from work then. By the look on his face, I knew something was wrong, but I wasn't sure what. I wasn't prepared for what he told me.

"Babe, I got fired today."

My heart immediately sank—I couldn't believe it. I began to sob uncontrollably as a panicked ache grew inside me. How were we going to take care of ourselves and our two little girls—*especially* our little girls?

Distinctly, through the Spirit, I heard, "Ask him how he's doing. He must be devastated."

Within a split second, my heart and mind changed.

I instantly stopped thinking about myself and our daughters and asked, "Are you okay?"

My husband's eyes filled with disbelief and shock—I knew he hadn't expected that question. Later he expressed the reason behind his look. He said, "I couldn't believe that after losing my job, which was my own fault, that you would be so forgiving and still love me. Anyone else would have left because I put them in financial danger and insecurity. The fact you chose to stay says a lot."

Through the prompting I received, I realized that what happened wasn't about *me*. It was about helping my husband know I would support him in everything we face—together.

Elder Dieter F. Uchtdorf said, "As you reach out to your Heavenly Father, as you pray to Him in the name of Christ, He will answer you. He speaks to us everywhere. . . . If you listen for the voice of the Father, He will lead you on a course that will allow you to experience the pure love of Christ."[2]

During that hard time, members of our ward gathered together in kindness, offering their emotional and financial support until my husband found another job. That was truly a blessing. But the biggest blessing for me came that day through the whisperings of the Spirit, when I heard the voice of the Father telling me to take care of my husband.

"Search diligently, pray always, and be believing, and all things shall work together for your good."

Doctrine and Covenants 90:24

11

TRUSTING HIM

"He shall consecrate thine afflictions for thy gain."
2 Nephi 2:2

◇◇

The apartment was cold with only a kerosene heater for warmth. The walls were growing green from the humidity. Using a small heater, I had just enough hot water for a quick shower. Handwashing was done with cold water, and my hands were chapped and dry. Woolen blankets provided warmth for my bed at night, though I thought the weight might flatten me into a pancake. Unfortunately, the blankets also provided warmth for the fleas. I learned that fleas bite and jump and bite again, and my legs and arms itched for relief.

I surveyed my surroundings with blurred vision at times—perhaps an eye infection. Although I had never had problems with asthma, I struggled to breathe during our long walks. Even the food was bad. The woman who cooked meals for us had a heavy hand with salt and grease. I prayed for relief.

Many months earlier, after a period of fasting and prayer, I had received heaven-sent direction through the Holy Ghost that I should serve a mission. I made the preparations and left for the Uruguay Montevideo mission in January 1976. I spent two months in the training mission to learn some basic Spanish and then flew to Uruguay. The city of Minas was my second assignment. My companion spoke only Spanish, and my Spanish improved as a result of constant practice. We got along well together. We knocked on every single door in Minas to spread the gospel message.

One day my companion began the door approach. The woman who answered the door replied that she did not speak English and started to close the door. Indignant, my companion stated that she was a native Uruguayan and was speaking Spanish.

"Perhaps, I wasn't listening," the woman said. Then she closed the door firmly. That seemed to happen at many of the doors . . . nobody wanted to hear about our message of Jesus Christ and His plan for our happiness.

Hungry and cold, flea-bitten, vision-challenged, and sometimes gasping for air, I wondered about my purpose as a missionary. After I shared my concerns with my mission president and asked for a change of location, he stated that I was exactly where God wanted me to be. I seriously considered going home. I knew God had wanted me to be a missionary, but I wondered if I would survive the experience. Would I perish in Uruguay?

After weeks of prayer and remembering the spiritual assurance that I should serve a mission, I made the decision.

I realized I needed to trust Him just like the scriptures teach. "Trust in the Lord with all thine heart; and lean not unto thine own understanding. In all thy ways acknowledge Him, and He shall direct thy paths" (Proverbs 3:5–6). Whatever happened, I was staying. I put my flea-bitten hand in the hand of God and promised Him I would work hard as a missionary—no matter what!

It was just a week later that I received a transfer to the capital city of Montevideo. I would be one of four sister missionaries to open up the city—there had not been sister missionaries in Montevideo for ten years.

I served in Uruguay for an additional nine months. Through our efforts preaching the gospel message, many people were baptized and lives were changed. I felt that I had reached a Gethsemane of my own in Minas, and I learned that giving the Lord a broken heart and contrite spirit can be the hardest thing of all . . . but the reward is heavenly.

"Spiritual worth means to value ourselves the way Heavenly Father values us, not as the world values us. Our worth was determined before we ever came to this earth."[1]

Joy D. Jones

12

HE LOVED ME FOR WHO I WAS

"Be still and know that I am God."
Psalm 46:10

◇◇

I grew up in Idaho as a member of The Church of Jesus Christ of Latter-day Saints. Since I was young, I remember hearing stories and testimonies of God answering prayers and people hearing promptings through the Holy Ghost. I yearned to have those experiences, but I didn't know what to do to have them or how a prompting from the Holy Ghost would feel. As a teenager, I would sometimes read Doctrine and Covenants 9:8–9 and wonder what that would be like: "If it is right I will cause that your bosom shall burn within you. . . . If it be not right you shall have no such feelings, but you shall have a stupor of thought."

The first time I heard Him was on my mission in Brazil.

I had been in Brazil for about a year. Several missionaries there were very successful, baptizing many individuals each transfer, and I didn't feel like I was measuring up. One transfer, my companion and I set unattainable goals for the number of lessons taught and converts baptized. I concluded that if goals help you realize success, and my goals were high, we should have more success in teaching and baptizing.

Partway through the transfer, we hadn't had any luck setting baptismal dates with our investigators—things kept falling through. I started getting discouraged. Since I was a farm boy from Idaho, the solution in my mind was to work harder. However, I discovered that working harder, contacting more people, and walking faster didn't help. Because I worried so much about numbers and about my performance compared to others, I became sick with a high fever. I stayed in the apartment to rest but continued thinking of all the work and possible baptisms I was missing out on.

By the second day, my fever had passed. I decided I could go on some visits and at least make our lunch appointment with a ward member. That morning, while getting ready for the day, I picked out one of my white shirts and started ironing it—something I had done many times before. As I was standing there in front of the ironing board, concentrating on getting the crease in the one of the sleeves just right, I felt—or heard—Him call me by name and say, "I love you. I know who you are and am aware of you."

I knew God had just spoken to me through the Holy Ghost. The feeling and the voice I heard were so vivid. In that moment, I realized it didn't matter how many people I taught or baptized on my mission—Heavenly Father knew me and loved me for who I was. What was more important was that I served Him to the best of my ability while teaching the people of Brazil.

"May we so live that our hearts are open at all times to the whisperings and comfort of the Spirit."[1]

James E. Faust

13

Acting in Faith

"Whosoever shall put their trust in God
shall be supported in their trials."
Alma 36:3

◇◇

In conversations with another member of the Church, I was introduced to a concept and some Church history I was unfamiliar with. As I "researched" it, I became more confused. The more research I did, the more questions and concerns I had. Things I had held as constant in my faith now seemed less certain. I continued to ponder and pray, but I could not figure it out.

Things came to a head. As I considered what to do, I turned to one of my favorite stories from President Boyd K. Packer:

> Shortly after I was called as a General Authority, I went to Elder Harold B. Lee for counsel. He listened very carefully to my problem and suggested that I see President David O. McKay. President McKay counseled me as to the direction I should go. I was very willing to be obedient but saw no way possible for me to do as he counseled me to do.

> I returned to Elder Lee and told him that I saw no way to move in the direction I was counseled to go. He said, 'The trouble with

you is you want to see the end from the beginning.' I replied that I would like to see at least a step or two ahead. Then came the lesson of a lifetime: 'You must learn to walk to the edge of the light, and then a few steps into the darkness; then the light will appear and show the way before you.' Then he quoted these 18 words from the Book of Mormon: "'Dispute not because ye see not, for ye receive no witness until after the trial of your faith' (Ether 12:6)."[2]

I decided I needed to shelf my concern and have faith that a resolution would come. I went on with my life, doing my best to act in faith—praying, studying, serving in my calling, and trying my best to live the gospel of Jesus Christ.

Several weeks later I was in my car, and the issue popped into my head again. It was followed by dialogue that played out in my mind:

Do you believe that the Book of Mormon is scripture? That it's the word of God?

I thought about it and concluded that I do.

Do you believe the Church of Jesus Christ has been restored?

Again, I thought about it and concluded I do.

Do you believe in a living prophet?

I do.

Then let it go.

I did.

Immediately, I felt totally at peace. The concern melted away. I had my answer.

That "issue" became a powerful faith-building experience for me. Since that time, I have had more witnesses of the truthfulness of the restored gospel of Jesus Christ. These witnesses have continued to strengthen my testimony and reinforce my beliefs and convictions that this is the Church of Jesus Christ and that I am on the right path to return to live with my Heavenly Father.

PART III

Hearing Him through Dreams, Visions, or Visitations

"Don't be fearful, and don't be discouraged. God will be with you on your journey always."[1]

Jeffrey R. Holland

14

HEAVENLY COMFORT

"Peace be unto the soul; thine adversity . . .
shall be but a small moment."
Doctrine and Covenants 121:7

Suddenly I awakened from a sound sleep. I wasn't sure why. The bedroom was quiet, my husband was sleeping, and everything around me seemed fine. Puzzled, I glanced at the clock on my nightstand—it read 4 a.m. In the next instant I realized what it was. Someone beyond the veil was in the room.

My first husband had died forty-five years earlier. When I realized the presence I was feeling was his, I started asking him questions in my mind: "Why are you here? What message do you have for me? Is this about one of our children?"

I did not get any clear impressions or answers back—I just felt his love for me and our family. Gradually, after about twenty minutes of being surrounded in comforting peace, he left. I had a hard time going back to sleep. Over the next several days, I reflected on his visit. Because of other similar experiences I'd had with him since he left this mortal existence, I felt something significant was going to happen.

A few weeks later, I traveled to California to spend ten days with my youngest sister for "girl time"—something we both look forward to and love. One evening, while we were making cards, I received a phone call from my daughter-in-law in Florida. She was crying and was difficult to understand. Finally, she was able to tell me, "He's gone," referring to her sixteen-year-old son, the youngest of her three children.

"Gone where?" I asked, feeling confused. I needed clarification.

She continued to cry. A few minutes later she told me he had died. I was so stunned I became speechless. Finally, I asked, "How?"

Her voice broke with raw pain. "He killed himself in his bedroom today after school."

My mind recoiled in disbelief. *My grandson died by suicide? Why?*

My daughter-in-law pleaded with me to come be with them as soon as I could. We talked for another several minutes on the telephone before she passed the call to her husband, my older son. He had a hard time sharing his feelings over what had happened in the past few hours. He also asked me to come. I told him I would as soon as I could make the travel arrangements.

After ending the call, I asked my brother-in-law for a priesthood blessing. This immediately brought me some comfort. Then I called my husband and told him about our grandson. We made travel plans for him to meet me in Florida. That relieved some of my worry.

I tried to sleep, but my mind was bombarded with thoughts. Pondering, reading, or singing the words of hymns is often a way I hear Him when I need help, and this is what I thought of:

> Where can I turn for peace? Where is my solace
> When other sources cease to make me whole? . . .
> Where, when my aching grows, Where, when I languish,
> Where, in my need to know, where can I run? . . .
> Where is the quiet hand to calm my anguish?
> Who, who can understand? He, only One.[1]

At 5:30 a.m. my daughter-in-law in Florida called again, pleading with me to come right away. I could feel her overwhelming grief and emotion as she repeated, "I need you and your son needs you." I told her I was coming as soon as I could get there.

Four of my grandchildren (two boys and two girls) were the same age. All four had been born within two months of each other. Now there were only three. I was concerned about how their cousin's suicide was going to affect each of them. Later that morning, one of them called me in tears. I tried to comfort him the best I could while dealing with my own deep heartache.

I arrived in Florida the next morning. My older son and his wife met me at the airport. They both poured out their anguish, and our tears flowed freely. My husband and younger son arrived that evening.

Over the next day and a half, more family members came from out of state—a total of thirteen, including the three sixteen-year-old grand-children. Two of my older son's best friends came—one from Utah and one from Arizona. My son kept saying he couldn't believe that all these people dropped everything and paid whatever it cost in order to come and support him and his family during this difficult time.

I too was gratefully overwhelmed by the love and support extended by their neighbors, members of their ward, and students from the high school my grandson had attended. I enjoyed listening to them talk about him and how he had impacted them through his kindness and friendli-ness. One high school student remembered his willingness to help any-one in class who was struggling with understanding the subject material. Others brought beautiful flowers, meals, and food items to their home.

The funeral was held at the church. The chapel was nearly full. I gave the opening prayer, and another family member read the eulogy. The bishop spoke, and then it was opened up for anyone to get up and talk. Our older son spoke. His heartfelt words and open grief over the loss of his son left most of the congregation in tears. He was followed by his two daughters, who shared tender memories and grief over the loss of their brother.

Teachers and many students from my grandson's high school shared memories as well. One of them described him as "a light that radiated through the classroom." The service ended with a talk about the plan of salvation. Nonmembers commented they could feel the Holy Spirit. The Relief Society prepared dinner for the family and close friends.

The next few days were filled with talking, reminiscing, crying,and occasional laughter—precious time spent together as an extended family before everyone started leaving for home. The goodbyes were heartfelt and full of strengthened love. I know the Lord was with us. We experi-enced His tender mercies during a time of tragedy.

By the time I got home, I was emotionally drained. I knew I needed to regroup and regain spiritual strength so I could be a support to all my family as they grieved and tried to adjust to this huge loss.

I reflected on feeling my deceased husband's presence just weeks before. Was my grandson's passing why he had come? I didn't know, but I do know that death is as much a part of our life as birth. Those beyond the veil have deep concern for us, and we will be together again.

More time passed, but still I struggled with the unsettledness my grandson's suicide left in my heart and the effect it was having on our family and friends. I fasted, prayed often, and went to the temple seeking comfort and peace. I did research, and I studied counsel from general authorities, yet I still couldn't come to terms with his suicide. I cried easily and was frustrated with how much I was still struggling. I had dealt with hard challenges in the past—the deaths of my first husband, my parents, a younger sister, and a son—but this death felt different.

Weeks later, I was again awakened early in the morning. The presence of my deceased husband was powerful. In my mind I asked him, "Why are you here? What did you come to tell me?"

After a little while, I sensed his answer.

He had come to let me know my grandson was fine and that they were together. Then I felt my grandson's presence too. My body was flooded with peace. I was able to visualize in my mind my deceased husband and other family members greeting my grandson warmly in the spirit world. I was comforted to know he was in good hands, surrounded by many who love him.

> He answers privately, Reaches my reaching
> In my Gethsemane, Savior and Friend.
> Gentle the peace he finds for my beseeching.
> Constant he is and kind, Love without end.[2]

Finally, healing had come.

*"Our hardships have
eternal purposes."*[1]

Donald L. Hallstrom

15

HE PARTED THE VEIL

"He appointed messengers . . .
to go forth and carry the light."
Doctrine and Covenants 138:30

The year my daughter turned eight and was going to be baptized was a tough year. A couple of months prior, my grandma had died. I was sad she was not going to be able to come to the baptism, but I knew she was happy and in a better place surrounded by family. I comforted myself by saying she would be there in spirit, but it was hard.

The night before the baptism, I got a phone call from my mom. She had a chronic disease and was not doing well. She told me she wouldn't be able to come to the baptism. I told her I understood, but inside I was devastated. I hung up the phone and cried. The two women who meant the most in my life would not be there for my daughter's baptism. Before I climbed into bed, I knelt in prayer, pouring out feelings of despair and disappointment to my Heavenly Father.

While I slept, I had a series of dreams.

In the first, I was at my daughter's baptism. I was sitting near the front of the room next to my daughter. As I glanced back to see who else had come, I saw my grandma enter. She looked directly at me and smiled before sitting down at the back of the room. The baptism started, so I couldn't get up to greet her. After it ended, I headed to where she had been, but she was gone.

In the next dream, I was at a missionary farewell for one of my sons, sitting on the stand next to him. My grandma entered the chapel, smiled at me, and again sat in the back. After the meeting was over, many people came up to talk, stopping me from getting to her before she left.

In the third dream, I was at a sealing of one of my children in the temple. Once again, just before the beginning of the sealing, Grandma walked in, smiled at me, and sat near the door. She was gone shortly after the sealing.

The final dream was at a baby blessing. Grandma was there again. She smiled at me and sat in the back. I wanted to talk to her, hug her, and let her know how much I loved her, but she had gone.

I woke up the morning of the baptism with peace.

I knew my grandma would be at all the major events in the lives of me and my children. Heavenly Father parted the veil for me that night to reassure me of this fact. "We can see His tender mercies and encouragement, especially in our trials, sorrows, and challenges, as well as our joys."[2] I was able to go through the baptism without sadness because of this beautiful gift from God. Hearing Him through this experience reminded me that He hears and answers our prayers.

"This very day—every day—He reaches out to you, desiring to heal you, to lift you up, and to replace the emptiness in your heart with an abiding joy."[1]

Dieter F. Uchtdorf

16

SCARS CAN BE REMINDERS OF MIRACLES

"Perfect love casteth out fear."
1 John 4:18

In 2019 my husband and I had received promptings that we should start growing our family. We fasted and prayed hard for a confirmation. We had wanted to wait a few years before having children, but we clearly received revelation that starting sooner was right. However, after two miscarriages and the accompanying intense heartbreak, I started doubting the Lord.

Why would you tell me I should have children right now if you won't even allow them to stay with me?

I heard many whispers during these difficult times that reminded me about the perfectness of His plan, and we continued trying with faith. When we got another positive pregnancy test, we were nervous, but we trusted and hoped that our precious baby would be able to physically join us this time.

When I was six weeks pregnant, I began getting extremely sick. I had the most intense abdominal pain I had ever felt in my life, which included violently vomiting multiple times an hour. After three visits to the emergency room, the doctors discovered I needed to have immediate surgery to remove my inflamed appendix that was about to burst. I was told by the doctors that the baby would most likely not make it through the surgery, but that if they didn't proceed, I could lose my own life as well.

My husband and I agreed to the surgery, and everything went better than expected. My pregnancy continued under close supervision. In 2020, that fighting soul I was carrying was born full-term without complications. We were so grateful to Heavenly Father for blessing us with our miracle daughter. But after her birth, despite my gratitude for the experience, I began to struggle.

Who was I now without my daughter inside me?

I felt like the "glow" from the miracles and blessings were all associated with her. I struggled with postpartum depression and anxiety. I felt I was just the vessel used to get her here, and upon her arrival I was thrown aside, left with literal and figurative scars of the past nine months from surgery, childbirth, anxiety, and fear.

A few weeks after the delivery, I started experiencing more excruciating abdominal pain. After many ER visits and doctor's appointments with no answers, an angel of a doctor decided to look deeper. She discovered that my gallbladder was full of stones, which was causing issues with my liver and pancreas. Once again, I was rushed into surgery, this time to remove my gallbladder. The surgery went well, but I now had three new surgical scars to add to my three previous ones and the stretch marks from childbirth.

While in the hospital, completely alone due to COVID-19 restrictions, I spent four long days with my thoughts. They became damaging and self-destructive. This was the darkest time of my entire life as I let those negative thoughts about my body become my reality.

The only reason your husband likes your body now is because he needs you to feed his baby. The mirror doesn't even show you how truly ugly and scarred you are now.

These thoughts and others like them consumed me. I hid from everyone, including myself and God.

For countless nights, I pled with Heavenly Father to send comfort and a change of heart, longing for the happy and confident me to come back. I battled moments of regret and anger for listening to the original promptings telling me to have a child, because in doing so, I felt like I lost myself. This was reinforced when people called and only asked about the baby. It seemed I wasn't wanted for *me* anymore—just for the daughter I had created.

I wanted my body back.

I wanted the scars gone.

I wanted things to be different.

Finally, one night I opened up completely to Heavenly Father about all my thoughts and feelings. I was very honest with Him and demanded to know what I needed to do to find myself and my worth again.

I could never have prepared myself for the answer I received.

He told me, "My daughter, I am so sorry you have been feeling this way. You are still important! You are still loved! You are still mine! You are not alone. I have been here at your side through this whole journey, even when you were mad at me and shut me out. Please remember that your Brother suffered these very moments for you, and He knows exactly what you are going through."

It was the first time in many months I felt a measure of peace.

That night I had the most beautiful dream—a continuation of the answer to my prayers. In the dream, I was sitting alone when I felt a hand on my shoulder. I turned around to see my Savior. He sat next to me and reached His hand in front of me with His palm up.

He said, "Scars can be ugly, but they can also be reminders of miracles. 'Behold, I have graven thee upon the palms of my hands' (1 Nephi 21:19). Even after being resurrected, I chose to keep these scars as a reminder of the pain you have felt and will feel in your life. I know what it's like to feel used and seen as unimportant. I know what it's like to feel alone. But I also know how important each one of us are to our Father's plan. He needed you to bring your daughter here, and He knew you would be able to handle these trials and learn from them. It will take time, but you will learn to see yourself as We see you. Remember that you were promised to have power over Satan, and that includes in your thoughts. He has no power over you. Your family, especially your husband, loves you. You are not a shell to be tossed aside when no longer needed—you are a vessel to bring great things to pass. See yourself as We see you, and love yourself as We love you." He gave me the biggest and most comforting hug while allowing me to sob in His arms, and then I woke up.

Today, I am not perfect in any way, but I have a new understanding of my worth as a daughter of God with infinite potential. By studying my patriarchal blessing, praying, communicating my feelings openly with my husband, and finding activities that help me feel like *me*, I have found an even greater love for myself and my body. I understand the impact the words I say about myself have on those around me, especially my daughter.

Because I was able to hear Him, I was able to turn one of the darkest, hardest, and loneliest times of my life into one of the greatest lessons I have ever learned. I have never been happier with myself or my life, and I believe this is because I needed to truly experience misery to fully experience joy. "All things have been done in the wisdom of him who knoweth all things" (2 Nephi 2:24).

"We can't fully appreciate joyful reunions later without tearful separations now. The only way to take sorrow out of death is to take love out of life."[1]

Russell M. Nelson

17

An Eternal Hug

"Fear not even unto death; for in this world
your joy is not full, but in me your joy is full."
Doctrine and Covenants 101:36

The year 2020 was a hard one . . . the year my life would change forever.

My dad was being cared for in a Veterans Home in Utah, six hours away. My family and I celebrated his seventy-third birthday with him. I didn't know it would be his last birthday here on earth. A couple days after we left, I felt guilty—he was having a hard time and preparing for an upcoming amputation. I told him I would be back for Easter break to visit. That made him excited.

The COVID-19 pandemic hit mid-March. Everything shut down, including the Veterans Home. My dad's health was declining. He had a second amputation in April, the day after Easter. He had now lost both of his feet, and I couldn't be there to comfort him. It was very difficult.

We talked on the phone every day and video chatted once a week, and I kept in touch with his nurses and doctor. I kept praying I would be able to go see him soon—hopefully for Father's Day—and that the pandemic would end.

In May, he grew worse.

We video chatted on a Monday. He was laughing, smiling, joking, and being his typical "firecracker" self. But a week later he looked older and pale. He had stopped eating, was on oxygen, and was tired and weak, alone in his room because of the pandemic. I hurt for him—being isolated was extra difficult because of his outgoing personality. On Thursday we talked a long time on the phone sharing special memories, and something felt different during our talk. That was the last meaningful conversation we had.

The next day I started feeling a "presence" in the room from the other side of the veil. Out of the corner of my eye, I caught glimpses of someone standing off to my side all throughout the day, but every time I shifted my gaze and focused on the spot, no one was there.

I didn't get to talk to my dad that whole weekend. Every time I called, he was asleep or not able to talk. I knew something wasn't right. I prayed to Heavenly Father to please let me know when my dad would go "home" and to help me to know what to do when that time came. The Veterans Home had told me they would let me know when I could come and say goodbye if they felt his time was getting close.

On Memorial Day, it was time for my weekly video chat with my dad. At 11:25 a.m. I got a call from his doctor. I assumed it was just an update, or maybe a call to tell me when I could go visit him, but it was neither. The doctor told me that at 11:11 a.m., my dad's heart had stopped when the nurse was checking him.

My dad was gone.

Immediately, I fell to my knees. "No—no—no!" I cried.

My husband took the phone from me to talk to the doctor while I sobbed. The instant wave of grief that assaulted me made my heart crumble—it was like part of me died. I cried out again. "Don't leave me! Please don't leave me!"

I lost my mom to cancer when I was fifteen. At the time, I told my dad that when he died, I needed him to let me know he was still close by, watching over me. I couldn't believe that time had come. I was only thirty-four and both my parents were gone from this earth. I didn't feel old enough to be experiencing this chapter in my life.

I had a lot of things to do, like taking care of my dad's property and possessions and making arrangements with the funeral home. It was hard to think clearly, let alone pack and get ready to leave the next day. My husband's parents were in town for the holiday, and my husband and father-in-law gave me a priesthood blessing. During the blessing, my husband's voice broke from emotion when he said, "Your dad will be waiting for you with arms outstretched to greet you."

This gave me great peace. Heavenly Father was answering my prayers. He knew what I needed.

That night I felt my dad directing me with things I needed to take care of for him. One included helping me remember the code to his safe, which I had forgotten. When I saw his physical body the next day at the funeral home, I was grateful he looked so peaceful. I felt him communicate with me. He let me know it was my mom whose presence I had felt a few days before. She had been preparing me for what was to come, and she had also been in the spirit world with my dad's parents to welcome him when he passed.

I felt him near while I packed up his things and took care of his belongings at his home. After I finished, I did one last walk-through in his apartment, stopping in his bedroom. All of a sudden, the ceiling light started flickering. The electricity passing through the three bulbs created a buzzing sound so loud that I wondered if the glass was going to shatter.

My dad, an electrician by trade, had just let me know he was in the room.

His presence was so strong that I started talking to him out loud. I felt his arms go around me, giving me a loving, warm hug. It was an incredible feeling to be held and finally get to say goodbye. My husband and kids heard me, and they came into the room and felt him there as well.

My dad was with me every day during the first month after he died. He talked to me. I heard his laugh. I felt his bubbly personality. His vibrant energy came through just as strong from the other side of the veil as it did when he was physically alive. I had many dreams about him, often waking up to feel him holding my hand. My kids experienced similar things. After that time, he came when I needed him, letting me know he was still around even when he was busy doing things on the other side.

***

A few months later, I experienced more deep heartache and pain from a different source, when my trust and ties to extended family were broken because of a significant trauma. I started having frequent panic attacks and chest pain. My hands shook, my head pounded, and it was hard to breathe—I thought I was going to have a heart attack. I felt shattered and betrayed. Multiple times I felt heavenly angels fill the room, and I knew some of them were family members. "In times of special need, He [sends] angels, divine messengers, to bless His children, reassure them that heaven [is] always very close and that His help [is] always very near."[2]

One day at my lowest point, I went to my bedroom, got down on my knees, and cried, "Please, Heavenly Father, please help me! Please—I need you. Please take this away."

The pain I was feeling inside from the heartache was terribly hard to bear. I felt like my life was broken. I wanted to crawl out of my body and skin just to make it stop. As I knelt there crying, begging my Heavenly Father for help, the room grew bright with a dense white cloud. Even though my eyes were closed, I could see it in my mind.

I felt my Heavenly Father wrap his arms around me and hold me tight. While he held me, I was enveloped in complete peace—as if I was no longer in my room. It was a feeling I didn't want to end. Then I heard Him say, "You are not alone. I hear you. You are a child of God. You are loved. I know your pain."

I realized I needed to let God be the judge of what had happened. I needed to forgive those who hurt me. If I didn't give up, and if I continued trusting Him in faith, the glory in the end would be unmeasurable. "For after much tribulation come the blessings" (Doctrine and Covenants 58:4).

I learned as I faced these hard trials that seemed too much to bear—the death of both parents and betrayal by those I loved—I did not have to be afraid. I have a Father in Heaven who loves me, a Savior who died for me, and an army of angels on the other side—all fighting for me.

Our loved ones aren't just gone when they leave this life through death. They are guarding and watching over us on the other side like an extra shield we feel but cannot see. "The veil of death is very thin. Those who have gone before are not strangers. . . . Loved ones may be just as close as the next room—separated only by the doors of death."[3]

I never would have imagined feeling closer to my dad after he passed away than when he was physically six hours from me on earth. Feeling him watching over me is special. I know I will always have hard trials—life is not easy. But knowing and having a testimony of my Savior gives me strength to fight the battles on earth until I receive that "eternal hug" on the other side.

PART IV

Hearing Him
through Others

"When we reach out to lift one another, we prove those powerful words: '[No one] goes his way alone.'"[1]

Ronald A. Rasband

18

SPIRITUAL NUTRITION

"Serve the Lord with gladness: come
before his presence with singing."
Psalm 100:2

I stood up during sacrament meeting as my name was announced from the pulpit. I'd been called as a new CTR7 teacher in Primary. Thankfully, the support looked unanimous, and as I sat back down, I heard a child's voice whisper loudly, "Mom, that's my new Primary teacher!"

Finally, after more than a year of the COVID-19 pandemic, Primary was to be up and running again.

A group of intensely and genuinely enthusiastic children were ready to sing together, ready to be in classrooms, and ready for something resembling normalcy. Well, as normal as it *could* be with masks and social distancing. Junior and senior Primary met as a single group, with children sitting in families for sharing time and singing time, rather than in classes. It wasn't until a few months later that we were allowed into a classroom with our own group of eight willing students.

During the time that church was limited to home study only, our three local wards were dissolved and combined into just two wards. All those holding callings were released, and each position had to be refilled. I went for about six months with no calling at all. It was difficult to create a connection with the members of my new ward, especially since there were many members I had never met before.

The *Come Follow Me* program helped me to hear Him. My gospel learning continued, and I felt close to the Lord and to my immediate family, even as I felt adrift from the congregation. Church on the couch became the norm. It was cozy and comfortable. As things began to open up again, members were able to choose to watch church from home or to attend in person. Then I was called as a Primary teacher—so no more church on the couch.

Being back in Primary for that first week was like culture shock. Not only were there adults and children that I didn't even know, but we were also all wearing masks. I felt frustrated and alone sitting in the Primary room. I was socially, emotionally, and spiritually distanced.

Little did I know that our Primary had been blessed with an exceptional music leader. Although she was a fellow member, she was a stranger to me, and I could see only her colorful dress, her long red hair, and her eyes—since the rest of her face was hidden behind her mask. As I settled in to half-heartedly sing the Primary songs I knew by rote, I could suddenly sense her heart as she enthusiastically led us. The words became dear and tender to me. I heard Him loud and clear through her and through the words of our well-worn Primary songs. In that moment, I felt transformed—childlike even—as my heart absorbed the spiritual nutrition the Lord provided me with. I was almost glad to be wearing a mask because it caught and hid my unexpected tears.

As much as those children looked forward to Primary each week, I looked forward even more to being there with them. My co-teacher and I often exchanged looks of delight and astonishment as we heard how much the children in our little class knew and loved the gospel. Every week I heard Him through them. I also looked forward to singing time with that special music leader. Each week as we finished singing, she would take a moment to look briefly into each child's eyes as she shared how much she loved being in Primary and singing with them. And even though she barely looked at the adults, my inner child felt like just as much a part of this weekly tradition. In those moments, I felt closer to God.

Now, a new year has come, I have new kids in my Primary class, and that amazing, red-haired sister was recently released as the music leader. And as I ponder these seemingly small yet exquisitely tender spiritual experiences, it's clear to me again and again that, most often, we hear Him through each other.

I hear Him through songs that testify of Christ, through the testimonies of children in Primary, through the talks in sacrament meeting, and through conversations with my husband, grown children, siblings, mother, and other family members. I hear Him through the kind words of friends, through my prayers and studies, and through the random smile of a stranger in the supermarket. And if I listen carefully, I can hear Him through all those within the sphere of my existence.

Because that's part of why we are here—to learn to hear Him through one another. And my hope is that others can also hear Him through me.

"Anchoring our souls to the Lord Jesus Christ requires listening to those He sends."[1]

Neil L. Andersen

19

BLESSINGS OF FAITH

"Faith cometh by hearing, and
hearing by the word of God."
Romans 10:17

Three weeks after I returned from my mission, I attended a young single adult dance in Roseville, California, where I met my future wife. We were introduced to each other, danced once, then danced again. I asked her for her telephone number, and we went on our first date shortly after. Soon we started spending as much time as possible together, and within five weeks, we decided we wanted to get married.

As we prepared, we discussed important topics. I was about to start my first semester in Rexburg at Brigham Young University–Idaho, and the decision of where we would live was fairly easy. We discussed how to handle potential situations and set some basic guidelines for our new growing relationship. We also discussed the topic of having children— how many we wanted and when we wanted to start having them. She wanted to have as many children as we were blessed with. I wanted to have one to three kids at the most. (She's the youngest of thirteen children, and I'm an only child.) We both agreed we would prayerfully make that decision later.

When we began discussing when we should start trying to have children, she said she was ready to start as soon as we were married. However, I was not. I wanted to wait until I finished my degree so I could focus on her and my education. I didn't want future children to suffer because I was at school and not able to spend a lot of time with them.

As we prepared for October general conference, I expressed my desire to listen with the question in mind of when should we have children. She readily agreed. I felt certain the Lord would say we should wait based on all the logical reasons I had convinced myself of.

Like so many other times in my life, I was wrong.

Elder Holland gave a wonderful talk entitled "Behold Thy Mother." Thankfully, I was in the right mindset and spirit as I listened to this talk. One thing Elder Holland said was, "No love in mortality comes closer to approximating the pure love of Jesus Christ than the selfless love a devoted mother has for her child."[2]

Immediately, when I heard that powerful statement, I received a direct prompting that brought me to tears. In my mind, I heard a voice ask, "Why would you deny this type of love from entering your home because you think you know better than Me?"

I was floored.

I have listened to conference several times in my life, always with questions or decisions I need help making. This was the only time I received an answer where I knew the Lord used a General Authority to speak directly to me. When I told my fiancée about the experience, she was excited I had finally caught up to her. She already had received her witness that we should start trying to have children as soon as we were married, and she had been waiting for me to receive a confirmation as well.

We were married that December. Six months later, we found out we were expecting. Our first daughter was born the following spring. Since then, her younger sister has joined our family as well. I can testify that the spirit that children bring into our home is unlike any other. I look forward to coming home after a hard day and having my girls run up to me with welcoming hugs and kisses. They help me get through difficult times with their constant positive attitudes and loving personalities. I am so grateful the Lord helped me hear Him and experience the joy of children early in my marriage.

"Kindness is the essence of greatness." [1]

Joseph B. Wirthlin

20

SWEET BREAD

"God does notice us, and he watches over us.
But it is usually through another person
that he meets our needs."[2]
Spencer W. Kimball

The news of my cousin's suicide came on a Wednesday morning. Nothing compares to the loss of a loved one—absolutely nothing.

It took a while for the shock to sink in. Before I could even start to do anything normal, like grab some clothes and hop in the shower, I said a prayer. I called up to God and asked Him to bring comfort to my aunt and uncle. I asked Him to bring comfort to my family. And I asked Him to bring me strength. I felt I needed to be able to be there for my parents and siblings because I knew this would be a pain they would all struggle to bear.

For the next three days, I could barely eat because grief overcame me, stealing my attention. By Saturday, I was on the other side of the country with the majority of my family to attend the funeral.

Up until then, all I had eaten was a hamburger at the airport on one of the layovers en route to my cousin's home several states away. It was late and I still didn't really feel like eating, but I did it because I knew I should.

Before the funeral service began, my family sat around talking. I was at the table with two of my cousins, an aunt, and my grandmother. Both my grandmother and younger cousin offered me a slice of sweet bread that was on the counter. I refused them both, deciding I didn't want to eat again—at least not until I had to.

Shortly after, another cousin also tried to get me to eat. He was much older than I was. We weren't close, and I hadn't seen him in several years. He slid the last slice of sweet bread over to me on a paper towel and told me to eat it. His attempt felt different—maybe because the others asked me or merely offered it, but he just *told* me.

Suddenly, in that moment, I felt seen.

I picked up the sweet bread and ate it. It was delicious. I didn't recognize it at the time, but that gave me the strength I had asked for in prayer days before. My cousin recognized something and gave me what I needed. The bread was simple—it didn't mean that much—but to me it was a lifeline I clung to. It was something I desperately needed during a time of loss and pain that had triggered me, making me spiral back to a place in my past when I'd had an unhealthy relationship with food.

I didn't skip a single meal the rest of the time I was away from home.

God used that small act of kindness from my cousin to remind me that He knew me and loved me—that sometimes hearing Him comes through the service of others.

Since then, the strongest parts of my grief have passed. That experience sparked a fight in me until I could get back to eating normally again. I'm pretty sure Gods' love had been kneaded into that bread—and courage must have been mixed in there as well.

*"God's answers are of eternal value.
They are worth the wait."*[1]

Dieter F. Uchtdorf

21

He Was Inspired

"Peace be unto thy soul; thine adversity and thine
afflictions shall be but a small moment."
Doctrine and Covenants 121:7

‹›

On one occasion, I felt the heavens were silent. My faith was sorely tested as we faced a horrible crisis situation in my family. It went on for days, weeks, and months, and at times I didn't know how much longer I could take it. I spent a lot of time on my knees in prayer. I fasted and counseled with priesthood leaders and medical professionals. I attended the temple regularly, and I studied to better understand what we were dealing with. After an especially hard day, I got down on my knees and sobbed, feeling completely discouraged, overwhelmed, and close to despair. I felt I'd done all I could, and I pled with God harder than ever before to send help.

Things became worse until one night it all came to a head and drastic measures became inevitable. My heartache grew as I had to make those difficult decisions, and during the next couple of weeks, I hurt, worried, questioned, and cried even more. But that night, unrecognized at first, the turning point had come. Slowly, little miracles began to happen. Glimpses of light broke through the darkness, and my trust in the Lord was strengthened again.

During the next stake conference, the stake president discussed adversity. The words of his talk were piercing, as if they were meant directly for me.

He said that sometimes when we are in the midst of a crisis, we may be praying, fasting, reading our scriptures, and going to church—doing all we can to be obedient and strong—but the heavens are silent. In reality Heavenly Father is there, but sometimes He pulls back to test our faith. Will we continue to be strong and obedient, or will we give up and turn away from Him? When we don't give up, the miracles start to happen and the blessings come.

His words testified to me of the truth concerning the recent challenge I had faced. I felt comfort in the reminder that God was with us the whole time, and I felt gratitude for an inspired stake president who shared a message I needed to hear.

The Apostle Peter wrote about a "trial of your faith, being much more precious than of gold" (1 Peter 1:7), and Jesus Christ said, "Satan hath desired to have you, that he may sift you as wheat: But I have prayed for thee, that thy faith fail not" (Luke 22: 31–32).

Trials of our faith make us stronger when we turn toward Him instead of away. "[For] it is upon the rock of our Redeemer, who is Christ, the Son of God, that ye must build your foundation; that when the devil shall send forth his mighty winds, yea, his shafts in the whirlwind, yea, when all his hail and his mighty storms shall beat upon you, it shall have no power over you to drag you down . . . because of the rock upon which ye are built" (Helaman 5:12).

"We cannot have true faith in the Lord without also having complete trust in the Lord's will and in the Lord's timing. As a result, no matter how strong our faith is, it cannot produce a result contrary to the will of Him in whom we have faith. Remember that when your prayers do not seem to be answered in the way or the time that you desire."[2]

"There is no obstacle too great, no challenge too difficult, that we cannot meet with faith."[1]

Gordon B. Hinckley

22

My Little Son

"For the Lord giveth wisdom: out of his mouth
come knowledge and understanding."
Proverbs 2:6

◇◇

When my twins were five years old, my husband and I were having severe struggles in our marriage. Both my husband and I worked full time, but it seemed like there was never enough money. As a mother of five children who was also maintaining a home, working, and serving in a demanding church calling, I was worn out. I never got enough sleep and felt short-tempered all the time. Trying to maintain everything was more than I could handle. As the months dragged by, I began thinking maybe the answer was divorce. That thought, however, caused me great sorrow and feelings of failure.

One Saturday, I was working in the backyard trying to get a handle on the weeds and mess. I was hot and tired. My husband and I planned to have a dinner later that evening away from the children to try and decide the course we should take for the future of our family. After finishing in the yard, I went into the house to get cleaned up and decided to take a bath to wash off the day's sweat and dirt.

As I was soaking in the tub, my youngest son came in, sat himself down on the closed toilet lid, and looked at me very intently.

"Mom, you love my dad, don't you?" he asked.

Taken by surprise, I thought about it and then truthfully answered, "Yes, I do love your daddy."

Very quietly he replied, "I love him too. I saw you and Daddy get married in that place. You know—the one with the guy on top of the building?"

"You mean the temple?"

His eyes lit up. "Yes, the temple!"

"The name of 'that guy' is the angel Moroni."

"That's it," he said. "I couldn't remember his name." He continued, "I was there, and so were my sisters and my brother."

Shivers went up my spine—I didn't know what to say next.

"Mommy, we were all there with you, and I know we're an eternal family."

I started to cry. My five-year-old baby was telling me "families are forever" as my husband and I were contemplating splitting our family apart.

He went on. "You know, Mommy, I was coming to earth but I forgot my twin sister and had to go back and get her. I couldn't come without her."

My tears fell faster. The year before their births, I had a miscarriage when I was about four months along. My husband knew this, but I had never told any of our children. We had waited a few months before trying again, and five months later I was pregnant with the twins.

My little boy's mind was opened to his life before he was born, and he shared with me that our family was eternal. In my heart, I heard Him whisper through the Spirit, "Fix this marriage. Work together to make things right. I've given you some insight—use it wisely."

We can hear Him in many different ways and means. And for me that day, it was through my little son.

*"He shall consecrate thine
afflictions for thy gain."*

2 Nephi 2:2

23

HEALING WITHIN LITTLE ARMS

*"He received them . . . and healed
them that had need of healing."
Luke 9:11*

I have anxiety, and after each of my pregnancies, postpartum depression hits me hard. During my second pregnancy, my husband and I had a text messaging conversation while he was at work that started some difficult feelings. I don't remember what the conversation was about, but something he said changed my mind and heart. Due to my anxiety, my mind started down a dark and negative path, which included suicidal thoughts. This included things like *He doesn't need me. Why does he love me? If I were gone, everyone would be happier.*

While I mentally wrestled, I looked at my sweet toddler. My gut wrenched thinking about what would happen to her if she discovered her mommy was gone. I grew extremely frightened and texted my husband again, telling him what I was struggling with. He responded immediately, telling to me to leave our daughter and go say a prayer in another room. This frightened me even more—I was afraid to be alone.

Sobbing, I took my daughter with me upstairs. She didn't know what was going on but continued to hold my hand and ask what was wrong. As I said a prayer through my tears, begging Heavenly Father to give me the strength I needed, my precious daughter held me in her arms and allowed me to sob. Who knew that within my daughter's arms I would feel the healing power of Christ's Atonement?

Dallin H. Oaks said, "Healing blessings come in many ways, each suited to our individual needs, as known to Him who loves us best."[1]

I am eternally grateful for the strength that my little daughter, my husband, and my Savior were able to give me that day.

"If you saw the size of the blessings coming, you would understand the magnitude of the battle you are fighting."

Author Unknown

24

HE WAS AWARE

"A man's heart deviseth his way:
but the Lord directeth his steps."
Proverbs 16:9

◇◇

My life was on a roller coaster ride. My husband and I had made a decision to get a divorce. Our marriage had been far from perfect— actually,
quite the opposite.

This was not the first time we had separated, but it was the hardest.
After our last separation, church brought us back together. We learned
to put Heavenly Father in our marriage. We became active in attending
all our meetings, committing to give it our all. We set the temple as our
goal, strived for it, and were sealed for time and all eternity.

Being here again, this time, was much harder. We had worked so
diligently only to fail again.

I had to face all of our friends. I had to go to church alone. I had
to explain to others what had happened. My heart was shattered. I felt
broken. I felt lost.

Divorce in many ways is like death, causing a lot of the same emotions like intense grief. I experienced that. The sadness seemed to stick
around—it clung to me. Thoughts of doubt overcame my mind.

Why am I living like this? Striving for perfection but always feeling like I'm coming up short or failing, wondering why I'm not worthy of being loved, and trying so hard to keep an eternal perspective?

Should I just give up and go back to my old lifestyle? Turn away from the Church, my covenants, and the gospel?

The "fiery darts of the adversary" (1 Nephi 15:24) we learn about in the Book of Mormon were flying and aimed right at me. What more would Satan love than to permanently break up my family? "[Satan] will never have a body, he will never have a wife or a family, and he will never have a fulness of joy, so he wants to make all men and women 'miserable like unto himself' (2 Nephi 2:27)."[1]

I recognized a war was raging, just like the scriptures teach. "He maketh war with the saints of God, and encompasseth them round about" (Doctrine and Covenants 76:29).

I knew I had to be deliberate in my actions while I struggled. I had to choose to "stand . . . in holy places and be not moved" (Doctrine and Covenants 87:8).

Although it was hard, every Sunday I kept going to church so I could feel a sense of renewal. I kept attending the temple as often as possible, and I kept my church family close.

One Sunday, I asked to speak to the bishop after church. He was aware of the situation between my husband and I, but I had not shared any of the doubts or questions that had been infiltrating my mind. He and I visited about life and how things were going. He mentioned he had noticed me crying often during sacrament meetings. During our conversation, he pointed to the large picture of the Savior in his office and told me He was the only person looking at me that I needed to worry about.

Near the end of our meeting, my bishop paused and said, "I feel prompted to share one last thing. I'm not sure why I'm telling you this, but don't give up! And don't go back to your old lifestyle."

The presence of the Spirit was tangible to me in that moment. I knew I was hearing Him. The bishop had not been aware of my specific thoughts, yet he clearly referenced them as if I had spoken them out loud. I had not told those thoughts to anyone. The Lord was more than aware of me and my struggles—I now knew that intimately. Tears rolled down my face as I received an immediate confirmation I was on the path the Lord intended for me. Giving up or turning away was *not* the answer.

My life wasn't falling apart—it was coming back together.

Within a few weeks, my husband and I began spending time together to try and figure out how to move forward. This included lots of time on our knees and in our bishop's office.

Ultimately, with the help of our loving, gracious Heavenly Father and the guidance of our bishop, we were able to mend our marriage.

PART V

HEARING HIM WHEN ATTENDING THE TEMPLE

"At the temple the dust of distraction seems to settle out, the fog and the haze seem to lift, and we can 'see' things that we were not able to see before and find a way through our troubles that we had not previously known."[1]

Boyd K. Packer

25

THE LORD KNEW

"Prove me now herewith . . . if I will not
open you the windows of heaven."
Malachi 3:10

While attending college, my wife and I and our growing family were not financially secure. Thankfully, we qualified for grants and scholarships, but still we struggled to make ends meet.

Twice a week I donated plasma. We used the money I earned to pay for our groceries. Each time I donated, I had to go through a screening process, which included getting my blood pressure checked. The stress from this process caused anxiety, which in turn increased my blood pressure reading, occasionally preventing donation. Whenever I couldn't donate plasma, I felt I was letting my wife down because we would not have as much to eat that week.

We both worked part-time jobs at a local call center conducting market research interviews, and we were at the top of our pay scale. However, we still didn't have the money we needed to make ends meet. We didn't have health insurance, and we constantly worried what we would do if our daughter got sick and needed to go to the doctor.

Friends encouraged us to apply for WIC, Medicaid, and Food Stamps. I immediately rejected the idea. I was raised in a home where "handouts" were discouraged, and I was ashamed that I wasn't providing better for my family. During this turmoil, I had a semester off from school. I told my wife I wanted to get a second job to help us make ends meet. I decided I would "pull myself up by my bootstraps" and make it work.

I found a job at a deli in the local grocery store. When the first paycheck came in, I was disappointed. Between both jobs, it still was not enough to support ourselves with the basics or put a little in savings. I changed my mind about applying for government aid, but inside I felt like a failure.

When we went to apply, I learned we were now making too *much* money to qualify because of the second job I had taken. I felt lost, like no matter what I did, I couldn't win.

My wife and I went to the temple to seek revelation from the Lord, to know what He would have us do to help the situation. While sitting in the celestial room, I received the distinct impression that I needed to talk to the manager at the grocery store and give my two weeks' notice.

I was dumbfounded. The Lord knew we needed *more* money, not less, and He was telling me to quit a job I had just started?

When I went to talk to my manager, I was extremely nervous. I explained the situation and told her I would not be able to continue working both jobs and that I'd have to quit the grocery store because it paid less. My manager listened intently, and I appreciated how understanding she was. She suggested that, instead of quitting, I should arrange my schedule to not work as many hours at the grocery store. I told her I would think about it and get back to her.

I discussed it with my wife, did the math, and discovered that it would work. We would be able to keep both jobs and still qualify for government aid. Heavenly Father knew it would work out. He had directed us to be able to provide for ourselves and still receive the help we needed.

***

A few months later, I was working as an intern in Utah, an important milestone for completing my degree. We found a family to rent from who agreed to reduce our rent in exchange for us doing improvements and maintenance on their house, which cut our monthly expenses in half. My wife and I painted, patched holes in walls, pruned the garden, trimmed hedges, shoveled snow, and anything else our landlady needed us to do. This helped us save a large portion of our income.

When we returned to Rexburg, I landed a job on campus working as a student support specialist for the BYU Pathway program. I loved it, and it was flexible with my class schedule. My day started at 3 a.m. I worked for a couple of hours, went to class, did a few more hours of work, and was home by 6 p.m. It was ideal and allowed me to have more time with my family—more than at any other point in my education. I loved the job, and the pay was what we needed to support our family with minimal government assistance.

On Wednesdays I was able to work eight to ten hours. This provided the largest chunk of our paycheck. One Wednesday morning while doing homework, I felt a massive pain in my groin as if I had been hit with a sledgehammer. Instantly I became shaky and queasy. The pain was so intense I was unable to focus on my homework any longer.

All day I lay in bed, feverish, with a temperature that climbed to 103 degrees. I tried to sleep off and on, but during the times I was coherent, I worried continuously, dwelling on how much money I was missing by not being at work. The next morning I went to the doctor. He sent me to the hospital five minutes away to get an ultrasound on my groin. No one was able to give me a clear diagnosis. I was grateful when the pain cleared up and my symptoms disappeared.

My next paycheck was much smaller. I logged onto the Church website to pay tithing like always, but my thoughts drifted to how hard it was now going to be to pay all of our bills if I did. I considered not paying my tithing, thinking I could just pay more later when we got a bigger check. During my hesitation, a clear impression came.

I *needed* to pay tithing. If I did, everything would work out—just as it had every time money had been tight.

I obeyed the prompting, though I still felt fearful. My wife's faith in being obedient was firmer. Three days later, we received a letter in the mail. It was from our landlady in Utah. She had been going over the records of all of the work we had done and realized there had been a clerical error. We had worked more hours than we had been compensated for. She included a check to cover the difference of what we were owed.

When I looked at the check, I broke down in tears. My wife couldn't figure out what was wrong. When I showed her the letter and the check, she joined with tears of her own. The amount of the check not only covered the money I didn't get when I missed the day of work—it exceeded it. I sent a prayer of gratitude heavenward. We cashed the check. We paid tithing on it, covered our bills, and had a little extra left over.

These two experiences helped cement my testimony of both personal revelation and the law of tithing. I know without a doubt that the Lord is aware of us and our needs, and when we hear Him and follow His direction, we are blessed.

"In certain moments, it can be difficult to see the hand of the Lord in our lives. But as we look back, we see how intricately He really was involved in the minute and challenging details."[1]

Becky Craven

26

THE SEALING ROOM WAS FILLED WITH LIGHT

*"Be thou humble; and the Lord thy God
shall lead thee by the hand, and give
thee answer to thy prayers."*
Doctrine and Covenants 112:10

◇◇

So many things had changed in my life, and I was desperately trying to
keep up. Now, God had brought me Trent. After my difficult divorce,
I seriously considered being done with men—for good. How much betrayal and pain could one person be expected to take? I didn't really
know—I just felt I had been given more than enough of my fair share,
plus being single had its advantages. Yet despite everything, I still believed in the God-ordained sanctity of marriage between a man and a
woman. I knew plenty of others who were happy in theirs, but I didn't
know if I would—or if I even wanted to—get married again.

Heavenly Father had a different plan.

About a month after my divorce was final, I came across a post Trent
had written on Facebook. We were both in a Latter-day Saints singles
group online, which was a resource for information regarding Church-
directed local activities in the area where I lived. I'm not sure why I

joined in the first place, except that I was lonely. COVID-19 isolation was raging, in-person church was no longer a thing at that time, and on the days I wasn't working, the clock ticked slower than ever. I didn't want to date anyone—I was too broken—but I did want someone to talk to who could relate to some of what I was experiencing.

Trent had written, "Through great trials can come unexpected truth and light."

The Spirit touched me through those words. I knew a lot about "great trials," and I also had experienced greater truth and light as I'd walked through them with the Lord. Trent's words piqued my interest, especially because the most important thing in my life was putting God first. As I looked at pictures and other posts on his page, it seemed like he shared the same priority. He had recently lost his wife after a two-year battle with cancer, and my heart hurt for him. I saw he was an author, something we had in common, and that he had just moved to Utah and was house-hunting. I had just finished that process and was closing on my new house in a few weeks. I looked up his book online, and it seemed like he had gone through a big transformation in his life. I was impressed.

I felt several times I should message him, but I ignored it because doing so felt awkward and uncomfortable. But when the feeling wouldn't go away, I finally listened and acted. My message to Trent was several paragraphs long, ending with wishing him luck on his house-hunting and saying that maybe our paths would cross sometime. His reply was two short sentences. I felt embarrassed for being so open, yet what I shared in the message had felt right.

Over the next few weeks, we started texting back and forth, and he clarified some things going on in his personal life that explained his initial response to me. His honesty was very comforting. I also ordered his book and read it.

At the end of the month, on my birthday, he asked me out.

I turned him down. I told him I wasn't dating—just looking for friends.

His response was that he didn't want to just be my friend—he wanted much more. That was scary for me because of all I had recently been through and was still dealing with in therapy. But I felt drawn to him.

We decided we would meet in person the following Sunday afternoon at a park to study *Come Follow Me* and have a picnic. I was adamant it wasn't a date—just hanging out as friends. I had a lot of healing to do. Granted, my heart was free and had been for a long time, but my emotions and mind were a mess. Trent told me he cared way more about my heart and that we could work through the rest together.

Our daily texting increased, and Trent began to occupy my thoughts. Something was definitely happening between us. One morning, a few days before our pre-arranged meeting, we decided we didn't want to wait any longer. We made plans to meet later that same afternoon. After that, we saw each other almost every day.

We had a lot to talk about and a lot to discover. Every time we were together, we prayed. We wanted to feel Him and hear Him—and we did. Miracles started happening, answers to prayers came clearly, and our love bloomed and grew. We were engaged a month later and married a month after that.

Along with many spiritual experiences and a strong confirmation that God had brought us together at that exact time, we also experienced opposition. "The adversary's greatest power is to give us fear, to tell us that what the Lord requires will be too uncomfortable, too impossible to do. But as we obey, the Lord will fill us with love and inexpressible joy."[2]

The suddenness of our intense relationship was hard for many people in our circle of family and friends, and they weren't quiet in their protests or opinions, especially a few very close to us. It hurt and created a struggle. In many ways, we understood. After all, if we had been giving advice to a friend or one of our adult children, we would have told them the same things—to take such a serious commitment slowly and not rush.

But for us, we knew God had other plans, and we knew we needed to listen. He taught us we needed to give others grace. Others weren't experiencing what we were, and He wanted us to trust Him and be obedient. We didn't necessarily understand His timing either, especially because both of us were still grieving—Trent over the recent loss of his first wife, and me from trauma and a recent divorce. Because our relationship was young, there would be a lot of growing together after we were husband and wife. We learned to "not question too much . . . for the God who ordained the beginning can be safely trusted with the end, as well as with all that lies in between."[3]

Because of COVID-19 restrictions, we were unable to be married and sealed in the temple at the same time. We had to be married civilly first and then sealed.

Since Trent was sealed to his first wife, I struggled with feeling "second." I knew I loved him, but I knew he had had a happy marriage for many years before God brought us together. On one hand, that was a comfort—he knew how to be truly committed and how to respect and honor a woman as his wife. But it was also hard not to wonder where I would fit. It was confusing at times, but Trent wanted to be sealed to me. When I prayed about it, I felt being sealed to him in the temple was what God wanted for us, but I struggled with my own mortal doubts and fears of truly belonging to him. I wrestled with understanding. "Until we subdue ourselves to the Lord, we can only experience frustration and pain. When we subdue ourselves to His will, we are filled with peace and dignity in all circumstances, no matter how challenging."[4]

I needed to get a cancellation of sealing from my previous husband before I could be sealed to Trent. This involved meeting with the bishop and the stake president and doing some paperwork. My ex-husband was also contacted in the process by my bishop and was asked to fill out some paperwork. I felt great anxiety during this time, but I'm grateful for Church leaders who were in tune with the Spirit. Once the former sealing was cancelled, Trent and I were able to schedule our sealing together in the temple within days.

The morning of our sealing was windy and cold, but we were glad it wasn't snowing. We had a one-hour drive to get to the temple. It felt a little surreal it was actually happening. I wished for the presence of extended family, but because of the timing and the ongoing pandemic, it didn't work out. I was grateful for the attendance of a few close friends, a daughter, and a son and his wife. As soon as the temple came into view, with its single central spire and stained glass windows, I felt overwhelmed with excitement and love for my husband and for the eternal covenants we were about to make.

Inside, as we knelt across the altar and looked into each other's eyes, I was filled with greater love and overwhelming peace. I heard Him reassure me I was exactly where I was supposed to be, and I was reminded He had brought Trent and I together. He had orchestrated all of it, and it was His blessing, His plan, for us. He had been telling me that all along the way despite everything—it all came down to where I chose to focus. It was my choice—to choose the joy—and now, in His house, He was giving it to me fully.

I received reassurance that my earlier doubts and fears were unfounded: I wasn't second to Trent's first wife—I was equal. The worries and fears I had fought, our initial concerns over getting married then sealed, others' opinions, the length of our courtship, my broken parts, and the past—all of it was swept away in the temple that day. He reminded me to "be still, and know that I am God" (Psalm 46:10).

I felt complete calm. My heart sang.

> Every long lost dream led me to where you are
> Others who broke my heart, they were like Northern stars
> Pointing me on the way into your loving arms
> This much I know is true
> That God blessed the broken road
> That led me straight to you."[5]

The sealing room was filled with light—*His* light—and it surrounded Trent and I in warmth. We had His promise and blessing at the beginning of our eternal marriage.

"Because He has experienced all our pains, afflictions, and infirmities, He knows how to help us rise above our daily difficulties."[1]

Cristina B. Franco

27

A Temple Blessing of Peace

*"In this sacred sanctuary, we will find peace;
we will be renewed and fortified."[2]*
Thomas S. Monson

The year 2000 brought great changes to my life.

I was taking care of my mother who was living with me. She was eighty-seven years old and recently diagnosed with acute myelogenous leukemia. Her health gradually deteriorated, and by June she was mostly bedridden. Because of her medical condition, her doctor recommended I use hospice to help provide palliative care. They arranged for a hospital bed to be delivered, which we put in the family room on the main floor of our home. It was much easier to care for her when I could raise and lower the bed. I was also grateful for the home health aides who came at least three days a week to bathe her.

Often I prayed fervently for heavenly help to give me the physical strength to care for my mother day and night—I couldn't do it on my own. Many nights I got very little sleep from getting up and down to meet her needs. She could not be left alone. My children were grown and living on their own, which left the responsibility on just me and my husband. When I needed to run errands, my husband stayed with her. This was challenging at times.

There were also times my mother was frustrated with her situation and became annoyed with me. Some days she wanted to get out of bed and go for a ride in the car. In order to do this, we would have to carry her out to the garage and lift her into the car, which included walking down several steps. The best alternative I could offer was to put her in the wheelchair and push her around the house or outside on the deck.

One day, just the two of us were home. After being up in the wheel-chair for a while, she told me she was tired of sitting and wanted to return to her bed. As I was getting her from the wheelchair to the bed, she slipped and we both ended up on the floor.

"How are you going to fix this?" she asked me.

"Actually, I'm not sure," I told her frankly.

We both started to laugh, then I started praying for help. We were relieved when I was given enough strength to get her up off the floor and safely back into bed, despite the fact she had no strength in her legs to help me. We experienced many instances like this when God answered our prayers.

As time passed, I learned to focus less on the challenges of caring for her and more on realizing it was a blessing to serve her during her last months in mortality. We shared many special, sweet moments together.

Eventually, my mother realized her time on this earth was coming to a close. Because my father and all her siblings were deceased, she started wondering—and even began to worry—how they would greet her when she passed. I tried to assure her they would welcome her with loving, open arms. She wrestled with these thoughts until the end, when she passed peacefully away on August 17, 2000.

After her death, as the weeks went by, I often wondered how she was doing and if she was happy. I prayed to somehow know the answer to my concern. One day, I went to the temple to attend an endowment session. I sat on the end of the second row next to the aisle. Every other seat on the sisters' side was eventually filled, but for some reason, no one sat in the last open seat on my left. I found this unusual.

As the session proceeded, I came to realize that seat actually was oc-cupied—by my mother. She communicated with me and let me know I didn't need to worry about her any more. She was doing well and she was very happy. Her sweet message touched my heart. I shed many tears during the session.

In the celestial room, the sister who sat on the other side of the "empty seat" came up to talk to me. She said, "I know there was someone in the seat between us. Do you know who it was?"

I told her, "Yes, it was my mother," and I gave her a little background information.

She gave me a hug and told me she had felt something special during the session, and it had been wonderful for her to have shared in the experience.

I know this experience in the temple was a tender mercy given to me by a loving Heavenly Father who recognized my need to know if my mother was doing well on the other side of the veil.

"[God] knows all the things we don't want anyone else to know about us—and loves us still."[1]

Gerrit W. Gong

28

The Temple Provided Direction

"I will not leave you comfortless: I will come to you."
John 14:18

My mom passed away from breast cancer when I was fifteen years old. It was very difficult. I hated that I lost out on so many things I wanted to share with her during that time in my life, like talking about boys, high school dances, and dress shopping. I also hated knowing she would be gone for bigger future milestones, like getting married and having children.

At age twenty, I got engaged to someone I had known since I was fourteen. He had been home from his mission for two weeks when he proposed. We chose to be married in the St. George Temple, a very special temple to me. It was my mom's favorite and the same one where she married my dad.

When I received my endowment, I had been praying I would feel my mom inside the temple and be able to talk with her. Ever since I was a little girl, I've believed the temple was the closest place to heaven on earth.

After the session ended, I found a secluded place in the celestial room to think about her and pray. I hoped she was there, so in my mind I asked her, "How do you feel about my fiancé? Do you approve? Do you think I'm marrying the right guy?"

Within moments, a temple worker came up to me with my fiancé in tow. She said, "I'm sorry to bother you, but I felt strongly I needed to bring him over to you, and I'm not sure why."

I realized my mom was letting me know she approved of him and was happy for me.

When I got married a week later, I saved a seat in the sealing room just for her. I knew that if there was an empty seat, she would come. During the sealing, I could feel the energy of her spirit radiating in the room. Even though I couldn't see her with my mortal eyes, I could feel her smile and her joy. When the ordinance was over, it was hard to leave since it was the closest I had felt to her since her death. I was so thankful my prayers were answered and that God let my mom come and be part of my wedding day.

A while later, I returned to the temple alone to do an endowment session. I felt my mom there again, and this time she was holding a baby. I was overwhelmed with emotion.

When I was in high school after my mom died, I fell apart. During that time, I got involved in a bad relationship that led to me being raped, resulting in pregnancy. I kept that deep, painful secret from my family because I was mad at myself for not being strong enough to leave the relationship sooner. I hated myself. At that time, I believed I would never be good enough to end up with a wonderful man or be married in the temple because of my mistake. I was sure my mom knew and was disappointed in me.

After I lost the baby, I met with my bishop. The meeting was very emotional, and the Spirit was strong. My bishop cried with me and told me I had been forgiven. I wondered how God could forgive me when I couldn't forgive myself, but I had prayed for a long time for His help. It was a turning point in my life.

I realized that the baby my mom was holding in the temple was the baby girl I had lost. Seeing them together brought me great comfort and peace. Finally, I was able to fully forgive myself after years of suffering. My baby was safe and knew I loved her, and she was being loved by my mom.

God and my mom both knew I needed that closure—and I received it in the temple.

We are promised, "The temple will provide direction . . . in a world filled with chaos. It is an eternal guidepost which will help you from getting lost in the 'mist of darkness.' It is the house of the Lord."[2]

I'm grateful the temple provided direction for me and cleared away the mist of darkness I was caught in from my painful past. I know that God knows me and loves me, and I know He never rejects us even when we struggle to forgive ourselves.

PART VI

HEARING HIM WHEN LED TO DO GOOD

"Because of the power He gives us as we are obedient, we are able to become more than we ever could on our own."[1]

Jean B. Bingham

29

SERVE GRACE

"Inasmuch as ye have done it unto the least of
these my brethren, ye have done it unto me."
Matthew 25:40

◇◇

Taking the family to Branson, Missouri, for a weekend of go-carts and goofing off doesn't usually include a singing waitress and a lesson from above regarding perspective. But then again, we were in the Christian live entertainment capital of the world.

After enjoying a day of fun at Silver Dollar City, we decided to have a meal at Mel's Hard Luck Café on our way out of town. Mel's is a fifties-themed diner with a unique attraction—all of the wait staff and owners are professional singers. In between refills, your waiter or waitress will stop what they are doing to perform a delightful rendition of a well-known gospel or country music song or an original song of their own.

It was at this Branson treasure that our family had a most unusual encounter. It started with the decision to share a decadent dessert as an appetizer: the "Peanut Butter, Banana, Raisin, and Caramel Concoction." My son was the first to finish his generous portion, and he made his way to the restroom to rid himself of the stickiness that is a side effect of this delightful treat. (Of course, you *could* use a knife and fork to avoid the mess, but if we had been that civilized, we would have missed out on an extremely valuable life lesson.)

As my son entered the restroom, an elderly couple waited outside the doorway. The wife politely asked my son if he would help her blind husband go inside. My son, usually eager to help, was a bit worried.

He asked, "You don't need me to go into the stall with him, do you?"

She replied, "No, just lead him to the door and he will be fine."

Relieved, he led the elderly man into the bathroom by the arm, guided him to the stall as requested, and then headed to the sink to scrub the remnants of the gooey treat from his hands.

After returning to the table, he didn't say anything about what had just occurred. However, when my wife returned, she did. She had witnessed his kindness. She had been behind him, also heading to the restroom to wash her hands. There is little in life that is more rewarding than the joy parents feel when their children make decisions to be decent and kind human beings, and to say I was joyful and happy would be an understatement.

The story could have ended there, with a son being a good example to his family on how to help others—very much like another Son, who is the greatest example in charity and kindness. But the life lesson our family received had another layer, or perspective, to it.

Our meals arrived, and we continued to enjoy wonderful live music from the talented restaurant staff. But now I needed to wash my own hands. When I entered the bathroom, I went right to the sink. I was stalled by a gentleman taking paper towels from the dispenser, drying his hands, and throwing them on the floor.

My first thought was *Wow, who does that?* Not only was he throwing the paper towels on the floor, but he was completely oblivious to the people around him, particularly to my need to wash up. His body blocked my access to the sink, and he was taking an incredible amount of time to perform the simple task of drying his own hands before going about his day.

What was probably thirty seconds to a minute seemed like an eternity as I continued to think about how much situational awareness was lacking in society today. Just as I was considering an aggressive tactic to rid myself of the gooey residue from my hands, the gentleman turned towards me and kindly asked if I would assist him to the door.

I was immediately humbled.

This was the same man my son had assisted to the restroom stall almost twenty minutes earlier. Sheepishly, I helped him to the door and returned him to his wife, who was patiently waiting outside the doorway.

I returned to the bathroom to wash my hands and then walked back to our table. I couldn't help but think how much this couple relied on the kindness of strangers to perform simple tasks I take for granted every day. The man was throwing the paper towels on the floor, but in hindsight, I realized he was throwing them where he thought the waste basket would be in relationship to the sink. Even with his disability, he was trying to be the best human being he could be. As I judged his situational awareness, could I say the same?

As I thought about my attitude toward this man—before realizing who he was and the limitations he faced with grace and dignity—I couldn't help but feel shame and regret for not being more considerate and understanding. When I realized this was the same man my son had helped, I was humbled by what I take for granted every day—the ability to use the bathroom in a timely manner without assistance.

Once I was removed from the situation and had time to reflect and ponder, the Spirit taught me there are opportunities to serve others in countless and simple ways throughout our everyday lives. Through these, we have the opportunity to serve Him and in some cases be an answer to prayer when we recognize this and take action.

Later I pondered more on this experience. It reminded me of a story I heard many years ago shared by a young mother in a talk at church. She had been given the assignment to bring a bowl of Jell-O to a potluck function. In the haste of life and the responsibilities she had, she didn't give the gelatin enough time to set properly. Not wanting to be late, she decided to bring it anyway, planning to put it in the refrigerator there to finish setting until it was time to eat.

On the drive to the event with her daughter, the Jell-O sloshed from side to side, threatening to escape the rim of the bowl with every turn or stop of the vehicle. In hopes of preventing a significant mess, she drove slowly and carefully, causing other drivers around her to react by honking their horns and signaling displeasure in a variety of ways.

The incident with the Jell-O created a new perspective. Ever since that day, when the young mother drove behind someone who was going slow or frustrating her progress on the road, she told herself, "They're probably trying to get to a potluck with a large bowl of unset gelatin."

When we go about our day in a hurry, and people in front of us slow our progress, we can instead focus on hearing Him by seeking to understand the challenge that person might be facing. Even if it is a situation of someone being inconsiderate, we can choose instead to serve a generous portion of His grace.

"Wherefore, be not weary in well-doing, for ye are laying the foundation of a great work. And out of small things proceedeth that which is great."

Doctrine and Covenants 64:33

30

I Can Open My Journal

"Trust God to lead you, even if that way looks different than you expected or is different from others."[1]
Michelle Craig

◇◇

After listening to an audiobook in the fall of 2019 suggesting the benefits of waking up early and following a specific routine, I was inspired to change.

I started waking up at 5 a.m., doing some form of cardio exercise for ten minutes, then spending thirty minutes in prayer and scripture study followed by twenty minutes of journaling. The most challenging part of the process was to record something meaningful. In fact, the first entry in my journal started with "I have no idea what to write, but . . ."

After a few days of struggling, I started to develop a pattern of decompressing the previous day's challenges, counting my blessings, and expressing my hopes or desires as well as challenges and concerns for the upcoming day or week. Within days, I found this process comforting and looked forward to it. Sometimes I could hardly write fast enough to capture all that I wanted to get out of my head.

After several weeks of thoughtful prayer, scripture study, and journal writing, a very specific question became persistent and common as I would write in my journal. The question was repeatedly impressed in my mind in a variety of ways but was basically the same: How should I be spending my time?

Like many, the requirements on my time were shared throughout several key areas of my life: the daily commitments as a father and husband; the responsibilities of a relatively new and challenging Church calling; the obligations as an owner of a growing business with employees and families to support; and lastly as a teacher, consultant, and professional speaker within a niche of the industry I work in.

As my journaling, prayers, and scripture study continued over the course of a few months, the answer to this question began to be impressed upon me and recorded within the pages of my journal.

As I pondered and sought to hear my Father in Heaven, specifically asking for His direction regarding how I should use my time, self-centered and prideful answers that had previously made their way into my journal were repeatedly overshadowed by an inspired answer that would take hold and cement itself as the true answer to my question.

At the end of February 2020, my answer was clear—I should focus my time on my family, Church calling, and core business. If the activity did not fit into one of these three areas of my life, I should not pursue it.

In order to follow this guidance, I had to let go of teaching, consulting, and speaking within my industry. This meant I had to say no during a busy season of upcoming requests for my time in this area.

These activities brought me great personal and professional satisfaction. They also contributed to my livelihood financially. Yet what I was most concerned about was how to explain this decision to the various people involved. I struggled with what people would think. My industry is a tight-knit community, and when I was no longer in the arena of teaching and presenting, would they think I was fired or led out to pasture?

I am grateful for a loving Father in Heaven who truly knows me and all my strengths and weaknesses. This decision was not easy, but it was important. Not only would it give me more time to focus on those three key areas of my life, but it would also help me get better at putting my ego and pride aside.

When I began to ponder my fears regarding this decision, it was clear that if I conquered those fears and had faith, God saw the opportunity for me to have a more joyful and rewarding life. This was part of the lesson He wanted me to learn.

He wanted me to serve my family, my brothers and sisters within my community, and my employees and clients in a greater and more meaningful way. He wanted me to become better at putting less important matters aside in order to have more time for more significant relationships and opportunities.

I made the difficult and necessary calls to let people know the decision I had made. To my surprise, people were very understanding and supportive. In some of these discussions, I was also able to share my testimony of personal revelation and the process of how I came to this decision.

In early March 2020, I boarded a flight to Amarillo, Texas, to consult with a company and complete one of the handful of the remaining commitments that would help me close this chapter of my life. The day I returned home from that trip, the entire world changed. The announcements of the COVID-19 pandemic and subsequent lockdowns was the discussion on every screen and in every publication. After I arrived home, I immediately shifted my energy to the safety of my family and employees, the health of my business, and the responsibilities within my Church calling.

Over the next few months, all the teaching, consulting, and professional speaking engagements were postponed and eventually canceled. The last remaining commitments, which I was not eager to complete, were taken off my plate.

Because I had made the decision to step away from these things even before they were taken from me, I did not grieve their loss. I celebrated the tender mercy of being able to focus my time in the areas of my life I had committed to, even earlier than I had anticipated.

By no longer traveling, teaching, and speaking, I have been able to build better relationships with the people in my life. It has allowed me to be present during challenging times within my immediate family, work family, and community. It has allowed me to focus more of my energy on growing my business and providing for my family and the families of my employees. It has allowed me to serve others in a more meaningful way than I had ever known before. It has also helped me strengthen my relationship with my Father in Heaven.

It's important to note that I am not trying to portray a story of perfection regarding how I spent my time after receiving this personal revelation. I would like to say that every hour was spent in a fruitful way, but that would not be true. I still allowed other less important matters to take me off course from time to time. In fact, there are many other distractions I still need to remove from my life as I strive to be more present with those who our Father in Heaven sends into my life.

I am grateful God gave me a formula to hear Him in my life. When an imbalance of time and misplaced priorities starts to take hold, I can open my journal and read the entries to remind myself what is most important and where I should be focusing my time.

"Embrace your sacred memories. Believe them. Write them down. Share them with your family. Trust that they come to you from your Heavenly Father and His Beloved Son. Let them bring patience to your doubts and understanding to your difficulties."[2]

"Offering forgiveness doesn't always heal the relationship. But offering forgiveness always enables God to heal your heart."

Author Unknown

31

FORGIVING IS HARD—NOT FORGIVING IS HARDER

*"For if ye forgive men their trespasses, your
heavenly Father will also forgive you."*
Matthew 6:14

◇◇

The sun was high in the summer sky, covering everything it touched in bright light as I walked along the vibrant foliage-filled pathway. Though I felt the golden rays on my skin, inside I wrestled with returning darkness. It was a darkness I longed to be free of, but how could I forgive something I couldn't forget?

Yes, there were times the hurt faded into the background and joy seeped in—until the next trigger hit. Then I'd feel the pain ooze from my pores, and a flood of tears would choke my breath in gasps. It was crazy how quickly it could happen and how deep it still ran. Repeatedly I felt the rejection, isolation, and loneliness from those I dearly loved who had abruptly torn themselves from my life. I reviewed it all in my head a thousand times, wondering how it could have happened. Why the sting of false accusations and betrayal still felt like a whip. How the trauma it caused could still bite so ferociously, driving me to my knees in surreal shock. How I wished I could become numb.

I wanted to truly heal, but I didn't know how. My prayers had been many and long, and yet I still waited for release. I desperately wanted off the emotional roller coaster I felt trapped on. I wanted to move forward in my life to a place where I could let go and choose joy more fully, regardless of others' choices.

Please God, make this stop. Please give me clarity and understanding, please restore what's been lost, or please increase my strength so I can bear it. Why is any measure of peace so fleeting?

I breathed in, hoping to catch the scent of a pale pink rosebush coming up on my left. My husband reached for my hand as we continued down the path, recognizing the struggle glistening in my eyes. His touch gave me a flash of comfort and respite from my thoughts. A bright orange butterfly flitted past and then landed on a juniper.

I wanted to forgive—but it felt so hard.

He looked at me and said, "Forgiveness is about love and, as you already know, turning toward Jesus Christ."

I felt puzzled. "Why do you say it's about love?" I queried, using my other hand to wipe beads of perspiration from the back of my neck. The air was warm.

He went on. "God tells us to love everyone, even those who hurt us. Whether we feel they deserve it or not, He says they do."

I knew the scripture in the New Testament well: "Love your enemies, bless them that curse you, do good to them that hate you, and pray for them which despitefully use you and persecute you" (Matthew 5:44). I understood that principle, and I knew forgiveness was right, but I was just so deep in the pain and the grief of loss that it was all I could feel or see.

Tears filled my eyes as we neared the end of our walk. Once we were back inside our home, my husband took me in his arms and reassured me of how loved I was, by him and by God. I was grateful for his comfort and kindness, but still my heart ached.

The next day we attended church. Second hour that week was Sunday school, and the lesson from *Come Follow Me* was about forgiveness. I felt intensely tuned in to the words of our instructor, especially when she shared a personal story about someone close to her who she struggled for years to forgive, and how much pain she felt because of his choices. She also shared how she felt when, finally, through an experience she had in the temple, she was able to forgive him completely. She talked about the blessings and peace that came as a result. She taught the class that forgiveness is about love and turning to Jesus Christ. Forgiveness is a commandment, and when we follow the commandments, blessings come.

Through her words that day, and my husband's words the day before, I heard Him. They had both spoken truth, and the Spirit witnessed that to me.

That experience helped me turn a corner. While it didn't end the grieving process over the loss of close relationships, or immediately heal the breaks in my heart, it set me more clearly on the path to finding lasting peace, for "living in the comfort of peace is so much better than living in the constraints of unforgiveness."[1]

Forgiveness is good, even though it's hard. Not forgiving is harder—because it steals peace. Jesus Christ knows about the pain of deep wounds, as He "was wounded in the house of [His] friends" (Zechariah 13:6). Giving my pain to Him helped me feel the light of His love, and that light filled me with hope and peace. The more hope and peace I had, the easier it became to have compassion for those who had hurt me. My eyes were opened with understanding to *their* pain—because hurt people hurt others.

Also, I learned that "to get better, you don't have to know why. Why they hurt you, why they misunderstood you, why they betrayed you. . . . Their reasons are multilayered with a mysterious mix of their own pain. But if you want to move on? Heal? Lay down what hurts? It's 100 percent your choice to make. Holding on to all the hurt will only steal from you all that's beautiful and possible for you. Let it go. Entrust it to God. He knows what happened and will address it all in equal measures of mercy and justice."[2]

"We grow closer to the Savior as we, out of pure love, serve others for Him."[1]

Henry B. Eyring

32

WE CONNECTED
THROUGH THE SPIRIT

"Small acts of charity have a healing
power for others and for [ourselves]."[2]
Silvia H. Allred

◇◇◇

It was past midnight. I stifled a yawn and finished charting at my computer in the nurse's station. In another hour, my shift would be half over.
The hospital corridor lights were dim, and it was relatively quiet since
most of the patients were sleeping. Things had gone smoothly so far. But
suddenly, my phone buzzed. It was the charge nurse letting me know I
would be getting a new patient soon—a woman who had just lost her
baby in the second trimester.

I reviewed her chart and checked with the nursing assistant to prepare her room. I also had to mentally prepare myself to care for her
emotionally when she arrived. Losing a baby was never easy, for the family or the staff assigned to their care. I thought back to the prayer I said
before my shift started—something I did before every shift. I enjoyed
my work—caring for moms and babies within a hospital setting—but I
knew I always needed His help to do my best in that role.

My patient arrived within the hour with her husband, strain and sadness evident in the eyes of both of them. My heart went out to them and their situation as I reviewed her orders from the doctor, got her settled, and did a routine exam. She was very sweet but tired. I let her know when I would be back to check on her again, made sure she could reach the call-light button, and quietly left her room.

A little later, after doing more charting and visiting my other patients, I returned to check on her. When I entered the room, I noticed her husband had left and she was alone. I could tell she had been crying and was in pain. She let me know she was ready for some medication. I left to get her some. When I returned, I logged into the computer, scanned her identification bracelet, and then scanned the medication. Before I gave it to her, I received a prompting that I needed to pray with her.

The prompting caught me by surprise. Normally I was very careful when caring for my patients to not bring up religion or spiritual topics unless *they* started that conversation. I was very aware of my role as a medical professional and the importance of having professional boundaries. I hesitated at the computer screen, contemplating how I should move forward.

The prompting came again.

I walked over to her, handed her the pain medication with a water cup, and waited for her to take it. She thanked me and swallowed the pills. Then I breathed in and asked, "Would you like me to pray with you?"

Her eyebrows raised in surprise and tears filled her eyes. "I would love that. Thank you so much. My husband needed to leave to go home to care for our other children, and I'm feeling really lonely . . . and sad."

I moved to kneel down by the side of her bed. The hard floor was cold through the thin fabric of my scrub pants, but warmth was growing in my heart. I reached for her hand and she clasped onto mine tightly. During the prayer, I asked Heavenly Father to bless her with comfort and peace, that she would know He was with her and that He was aware of her needs, especially during this time of difficulty and loss.

We cried together.

We connected through the Spirit.

I felt grateful for the opportunity I had to be her nurse that night— that I was able to hear Him and be there for her to offer comfort and support in a way different from my usual patient care. My own concerns were lightened through serving her—for Him.

"In all of our service, we need to be sensitive to the promptings of the Holy Ghost. The still, small voice will let us know who needs our help and what we can do to help them."[3]

PART VII

Hearing Him When Healing from Abuse or Mental Illness

"Through the redeeming Atonement and glorious Resurrection of Jesus Christ, broken hearts can be healed, anguish can become peace, and distress can become hope."[1]

Reyna Aburto

33

LONELY BUT NOT ALONE

"Look unto me in every thought;
doubt not, fear not."
Doctrine and Covenants 6:36

I watched her blue eyes widen with disbelief, dark eyebrows arching above, as soon as we were alone. "Can't you see he's abusing you?" she blurted, shaking her head as if incredulously daring me to disagree.

The conversation she recently witnessed between my husband and me hung in the air between us. The words he had thrown my way before he left were hurtful but nothing I hadn't heard before—behind closed doors. I was surprised at his boldness in front of her, but lately his anger had been less controlled, especially when I remained calm. My lack of reaction only incited his own, often escalating it.

I looked at her in silence as part of me recoiled. No longer could I feel the late afternoon sunlight streaming through the living room window. Instead, as I battled internally, I felt an icy assault inside, like a blowing snowstorm that steals one's breath.

Abuse? Did that word fit my marriage? My husband was a lot of things, but I had never labeled him *that* way. And besides, my train of thought tried to reason, he'd never hit me.

Several emotions crossed her face while years of memories began flooding my mind—both of us caught in varying degrees of realization and pain. When her eyes began to glisten with tears, she turned and left the room before they fell.

My thoughts took off over the next days, weeks, and months. As my mind was opened and I was taught by the Spirit, many things were brought to my recollection. I began seeing what I never had before. "And by the power of the Holy Ghost ye may know the truth of all things" (Moroni 10:5).

Times too numerous to count, I had excused my husband's behavior, blaming myself for saying and doing the wrong thing first. I told myself I should keep working on being more forgiving. After all, our marriage was supposed to be forever—a work in progress—and I had imperfections of my own. I read numerous self-help books, we had regular date nights, and we celebrated anniversaries with weekend getaways alone. I utilized prayer endlessly, asking God for direction, guidance, peace, and increased love, and then acted on the answers I received. And there *were* good times, even if they never lasted as long as I hoped.

But as time passed and our children grew up and moved out, I realized I was breaking inside. I felt nothing I did was ever enough. I was scared of my husband's anger, which he shifted to me and then blamed me for causing.

I cried often—usually alone. His most common reaction was to ignore it and walk away, completely lacking empathy about my expressed heartache. When I tried to talk about it logically and share it, desperately wanting to be heard and understood, it became a contest of sorts and, according to him, he had it worse. He frequently deflected my openness and made it all about himself, saying he was actually the one unloved, misunderstood, neglected, and ignored. My growing frustration of not having any resolution increased my feelings of isolation.

Many days I tried to stop feeling anything to make coping easier, but the pain was deep and I could only block it for a time before it overflowed again, drenching me in its jagged sharpness. I had reoccurring suicidal thoughts. When I told him about this, his concern seemed shallow, and later he used my vulnerable words to tell me I was mentally unstable. If I shut down to self-protective mode, unable to communicate, he seemed to figure out he had pushed too far. If that happened, he might offer a rare apology, tell me he loved me, and say how much he wanted our marriage to work.

I felt confused.

We tried counseling for several months. On the way home after some sessions, he was upset because I had openly shared what he and I were struggling with—the whole point of going. He told me I had betrayed him. During other sessions, he disagreed with the counselor, arguing against the advice he gave us. I was frustrated we weren't progressing as a couple the way I had hoped. But in actuality, a change was occurring *inside* me.

Like a light switching on, I started to see my husband and our marriage with new clarity. Sometimes you don't know *what* you don't know *until* you know—and then you can never go back to not knowing. Gradually, my husband's abusive behavior had become my normal, which is why I hadn't realized what it was. But eventually, the disarrayed dominoes of my life became lined up through a series of intertwined, multi-layered experiences, and once the dominoes began to fall, nothing could stop them.

I *was* being abused.

My mind fought to comprehend that *that* word now described me. For months I had been operating on autopilot, especially at work, regarding the almost constant hurt and unhappiness I struggled with. I knew that if I let my thoughts wander to my reality, an uncontrollable floodgate would open, possibly washing me away. It wasn't until much later, when I began to heal, that I could see that the Lord—for even longer than I knew—had been guiding my choices to prepare to face it.

If I was honest, I realized I did not love my husband anymore the way a wife should. I hadn't for a long time—he had hurt me too much.

I didn't trust him—there had been too many lies.

I didn't respect him—he had belittled me to the point I frequently questioned my worth.

Yet comprehension on how to move forward eluded me because I was so afraid.

Afraid of him. Afraid of leaving. Afraid of staying. Afraid of being with him—especially for forever. Afraid of being alone. Afraid of an ugly divorce and how it would affect our children. Afraid of an unknown future. And on and on. Because of where I was mentally and emotionally, fear held me captive. But fear is a liar, and it doesn't come from God. The scriptures tell us, "Look unto me in every thought; doubt not, fear not" (Doctrine and Covenants 6:36).

One night, an attempt of reconnection with my husband turned into an argument when I wouldn't comply with his wishes. The abusive words he hurled were so degrading that my mind could barely comprehend they had come from his lips. They tore me so deeply emotionally that it felt like they should have visibly scarred my face.

The next day, I moved out of the master bedroom and into my office, still reeling. Late in the afternoon, after many more tears, I found enough courage to make a desperate phone call to someone I could trust. The advice I was given was to pray and ask Heavenly Father if I needed to leave my husband. To some, the answer to that question would have been obvious, but for me it hadn't yet come. I don't know why, except maybe I hadn't been ready. Before I went to bed, I prayed and asked.

The next morning, I was up at 5:15 a.m. to prepare for another twelve-hour shift at the hospital. I had tossed and turned most of the night, but the blaring alarm on my desk had no mercy. During the morning commute, my thoughts returned to the night before and to all my fears. The heavens were silent, but I prayed again. I prayed for strength and direction, knowing it would come and dreading it at the same time.

What if my marriage was over? Could I continue living—existing this way—if it wasn't? Confusion and doubts dominated my heart.

The beginning of my shift was as hectic as always—getting my assignment, receiving the report from the off-going nurse, making rounds on my patients, and charting. It didn't slow down until about 10:30 a.m. when I took a short break. I was skimming an article on the Church website on my phone when I heard God through a distinct voice in my mind. Tears immediately filled my eyes. His words were clear, but my heart strove to understand *how* to do what He told me to.

The answer to my prayer wasn't at all what I had expected. Nor did I realize that *that* answer *would* set in motion the end of my marriage. It wasn't time for me to know—I had more learning and growing to do. But I did know I could trust Him. He knew exactly what I was facing and what I needed, and He confirmed once again that He was walking with me.

Over the next few days, more spiritual promptings came—answers in the form of thoughts and feelings. I knew I needed to physically separate from my husband, and I knew he wouldn't agree to move out of our home, which meant I had to. I wrestled with how and where to go. I tried different solutions, but when they ended up as dead-ends, I questioned if I was really hearing Him. Still, the prompting to leave kept coming.

At the end of the week, I had a few days off work—a small window of time I could feasibly move out and get somewhat settled—but I still didn't know where to move. I felt I was to prepare to leave anyway. I packed when my husband was out of the house, putting things in my car and in my office, afraid that if he knew I was leaving, he would try to stop me. I had feelings to take certain things—items I wouldn't have thought of on my own.

Inside me, anxiety raged. I was barely eating or sleeping, battling constant nausea, and crying for hours off and on during the day—trying to believe I was actually leaving my husband and home and filled with questions about what would come next.

Down to the day before I knew I was supposed to leave, I still hadn't found a place to go, as each option I considered or moved toward became another dead end. Previously I had looked online at the Airbnb website, but the few possibilities there had not worked out. I felt like I should look again. This time, I came across a new listing about a half hour away in a nice but unfamiliar area. As I read through the description, I received a calm feeling followed by the thought, *You will be safe there.* I immediately reached out to the owner requesting to book it for the next thirty days. I continued packing through the afternoon, frequently checking my phone to see if the response had come.

At about 11:30 p.m. I finally heard back. My request had been declined. The owner said the basement suite had already been rented and was sorry it had been relisted by mistake. I was discouraged, certain that that was where I was supposed to go based on the prompting I had received earlier. Tears fell as I prayed about it again. The answer I received was to trust Him.

I didn't know what to do next. I was now hours away from needing to leave, with still no place to go. It was after midnight, yet I couldn't sleep. I started searching again on the Airbnb website, hoping there was another place I may have missed.

The original listing kept coming back to my mind—it still felt like that was where I was supposed to be. I reached out to the owner again, this time explaining my situation in a little more detail—telling her I was separating from my husband and needed a safe place while I could figure out what to do. It was hard being open and vulnerable to a stranger. I asked her if she had anything else available that I could rent. I pushed send, wiped my tears, and prayed again before falling asleep exhausted. I woke up less than two hours later and checked my phone. I knew the owner was probably asleep, but I was restless and worried and kept checking every few hours anyway. Around 9 a.m. I got a response.

She told me she would be willing to rent out a bedroom in the main part of her house with a private bath if I didn't mind sharing the kitchen, and that there was space in her garage for my car. She quoted a price I felt I could manage. She said she didn't usually rent out rooms in her own living space but wanted to help me. She had recently gone through her own divorce and knew what a difficult time it was.

The Spirit confirmed to me that it was where I was supposed to be.

I messaged back, thanked her, and told her I wanted the room. She said it would be clean and ready that afternoon. Despite my anxiety of what the next several hours would bring—final packing, telling my husband I was leaving, then actually leaving—I felt reassurance from God.

Later that night, in a strange bed, in a strange house, in an unfamiliar neighborhood, I cried myself to sleep—a little less scared.

I had done it. I had left.

Despite how hard it was, despite not knowing what would happen next, despite a million reasons why I didn't want to face what I was facing, I knew the Lord had led me to that exact spot at that exact time. He had heard my prayers and had answered them in His way and in His time. He promises us, "Fear thou not; for I am with thee: be not dismayed; for I am thy God: I will strengthen thee; yea, I will help thee" (Isaiah 41:10).

I was lonely—but not alone.

***

The next morning, I received a long text from my husband. My leaving had gotten his attention. He told me he wanted to change and be accountable for the things he had done to me and our children. He said he knew he needed help and told me he was starting intensive therapy. His first appointment was the following day.

His words cracked open a tiny space of hope inside my bruised and battered heart, but the pain he had inflicted for so long greatly overshadowed it. I knew the only one I could truly trust was God, and I was determined to do all I could to keep hearing Him to see how things would unfold.

I had wonderful support from extended family and friends during this difficult time. I felt God's love through them and continued to receive His guidance through prayer, attending the temple, and counseling with my Church leaders. My mind also became clearer about more things that had occurred in the past. While the reality of what it meant was hard to comprehend, this time of separation from my husband taught me a lot. I learned I was not responsible for what my husband had said or done over the years, regardless of the countless times he tried to shift blame to me and our children. I was only responsible for my own words, choices, actions, and behavior. That was a big thing for me.

Repeatedly during this time, I saw and felt God guiding me on a daily basis as He filled my mind with specific directions of what I should do, where I should go, and who I could trust. He also helped me become more independent and self-sufficient, something I needed to get better at to face what was coming. He understood I needed a "trial run" to realize I had more strength than I knew and to reconfirm that He was walking with me in all of it.

After many weeks of separation, I received another prompting that it was time to return home to a separate wing of our house and try again with my husband. The Lord let me know that I needed to see if the changes my husband said he was making were real. I had also started therapy, which helped me realize how extensive the damage from the abuse was.

Upon my return, things went well at first, but underneath the surface I felt lingering uncertainties. My husband initially seemed better at guarding his words, but in his eyes, I got flashes of simmering negative energy that put all my senses on guard. But I knew it took time to change, and there seemed to be some progress, so I continued to hang on to hope.

One night, a discussion led to an argument and his anger flared. Though it was more controlled than in the past, he started blaming and accusing me of things *he* had actually done. I quickly left that part of the house, entered what was now my own bedroom, and locked the door. That barrier was more than literal. Where before I had begun to reopen myself up to him, feeling some warmth through recent conversations and shared experiences, I had now emotionally and physically shifted to emptiness.

I discussed the shift with my therapist and with my husband. We started couples therapy as a last resort. Though that helped us discuss some underlying issues, something big didn't feel right, and things at home in our relationship were up and down. I returned again to the temple, searching to feel any peace about staying with him—because of the covenants we'd made there, because of our children, because of how long I'd invested in the relationship, and because he said he wanted to change. I cried through most of the session, feeling turmoil. I left feeling 98% sure a divorce was the direction I needed to go, but I wouldn't take that final step until I was at 100%.

We met with the stake president together. He gave priesthood blessings to both my husband and me. In that blessing, I was promised I would know *for sure* what direction I needed to take. That comforted my heart, though my mind still wasn't sure.

Three days later, after a revealing conversation we had together with our bishop in his office, I knew. After I had agonized for months, it was as if the final piece of a puzzle finally showed itself and clicked into place.

Our marriage was over. I knew it for sure. God had accepted my sacrifice.

Heavenly Father reassured me that He loved me and that it was okay for me to go. It was time for me to move forward to a place in my life where I could end the recurring pain, heal, and find peace. I learned that sometimes God restores our broken relationships, and sometimes He rescues us from them. For me, I needed rescuing. He was with me through the entire process, and I knew He would help me to eventually forgive.

The Lord says, "I, the Lord, will forgive whom I will forgive, but of you it is required to forgive all men" (Doctrine and Covenants 64:10). Elder Holland clarifies, "It is important for some of you living in real anguish to note what He did *not* say. He did *not* say, 'You are not allowed to feel true pain or real sorrow from the shattering experiences you have had at the hand of another.' *Nor* did He say, 'In order to forgive fully, you have to reenter a toxic relationship or return to an abusive, destructive circumstance.' But notwithstanding even the most terrible offenses that might come to us, we can rise above our pain only when we put our feet onto the path of true healing."[1]

I know that path is the one walked by our Savior, and He calls to each of us, "Come, follow me" (Luke 18:22).

"The cavity which suffering carves into our souls will one day also be the receptacle of joy."[1]

Neal A. Maxwell

34

HE WAS THERE ALL ALONG

"With his stripes we are healed."
Isaiah 53:5

◇◇◇

Growing up, I gained a great love and appreciation for my Savior early on. I seemed to easily grasp the concept of His sacrifice for me and what it should mean in my life. At the age of twelve, the gospel became front and center of everything I did. I desperately held on to it as much as I could. At the time, I felt I could hear Him clearly and know what He had planned for my future.

As I moved into my years of middle school and then high school, that voice slowly faded away in my mind. I was utterly confused at my circumstances and all I had to uphold on a daily basis. I was never able to "catch a break" as my mind was flooded with memories I couldn't block any longer.

Experiences I'd had as a child began preventing me from moving forward in my life. I frequently endured long nights of crying myself to sleep, remembering the pain and wanting to escape. I felt numb to joy—nothing mattered to me anymore. Day after day, I tried to survive the emotions that my brain couldn't process from my past. Waves of inadequacy, anxiety, and fear crippled my life. I dreaded waking up in the morning—another reminder I had no control over my life—and could find no peace. I came to a point when I truly believed I had nothing to contribute to the world and was left wandering with no purpose.

In my junior year of high school, I decided I needed help, finally resigned to the fact I could not fix this on my own. All I could think about was how I would never measure up, whether to God's expectations or to the people around me. I felt weighed down by pressure.

I decided to start seeing a therapist.

Soon I was diagnosed with severe Post-Traumatic Stress Disorder and Major Depressive Disorder. This put me in a 1% category of teenagers who had these severe diagnoses.

I felt hopeless and empty—like my future fate had been decided. How could I ever overcome this sorrow and pain that I was experiencing? I was angry. Where was God in all this? Did He even care about me?

I spent a long time trying to control my circumstances. I subtracted God from the equation and continued to ignore the spiritual experiences I had when I was younger. I was determined to do everything by myself. I didn't ask for help because I truly believed I could do it all.

In working with my therapist, I started practicing EMDR—Eye Movement Desensitization and Reprocessing. My therapist taught me how to think differently about my past. I was able to find the root of why I had been feeling so overpowered for so long.

Slowly, I started to feel hopeful again, like there was a slight glimmer of light at the end of the tunnel. Day-to-day living was still really hard, but I decided it was time to let God back into my life. Little by little, I started listening to the promptings He'd been giving me the whole time. I let myself trust that if anyone could help me through this, it was Him.

Years later, I have come to recognize that God was speaking to me during that entire time in my life. Every day, He answered the small prayers I sent heavenward to keep me going. When I cried and begged for help to understand why it was happening to me, He reassured me. His love and grace saved me from a worse fate.

Today I am overwhelmed with gratitude to my Heavenly Father. I know I can never repay Him for all He has blessed me with in this life. I stand in awe of the true, raw power of the Atonement of our Savior Jesus Christ. There is nothing we will go through in this life that the Lord can't pull us through.

I'm thankful for the times God let me feel the pain—the times He let me struggle to move forward. In those times I learned to push, to really work hard, and to trust Him. It's because of the hard times I've experienced in my life that I see people differently than I did before. It's because of what I've gone through that I can offer empathy. I can feel love for those around me when I see them through God's eyes. I am grateful for this new perspective in my life and how I've learned to hear Him.

*"Wait on the Lord: be of good courage,
and he shall strengthen thine heart."*

Psalm 27: 14

35

THE PROCESS OF BEING HEALED

"And I will also ease the burdens which are put upon
your shoulders . . . that ye may know of a surety that I,
the Lord God, do visit my people in their afflictions."
Mosiah 24:14

◇◇

"Let God prevail."[1]

Like many others, I heard this counsel spoken by President Russell M. Nelson in the October 2020 general conference. To me, these three words mean handing over your will to God, having the patience to let His timing unfold, and remembering who to have faith in. At the time I heard this counsel, I was rocking in a rocking chair—the same way I had for weeks, even months, hoping my circumstances would change.

In January of 2020, the beginning of that year, I suffered a mental breakdown.

I had worked night shifts almost exclusively for over ten years in downtown Portland. Two hours into my first shift as a police officer, my trainer and I responded to a shooting outside a club where a fifteen-year-old fired about ten rounds at a moving car. We arrested him. On my second shift, a young man killed himself in a hotel room where his former girlfriend was getting married. He wore a plain white shirt with her name and the words "I love you" written on the front. We found him lying in a pool of blood next to the firearm he had used.

Over a decade of my life has been spent in law enforcement, dealing with numerous similar events and horrible things that most of society is oblivious to, *allowing* them to view life through a more positive lens.

As policies in policing changed and officers were no longer on the offensive, it became nearly impossible to be effective in preventing and handling crime. We could no longer take care of society—just put band-aids everywhere. Years of talking people down from bridges, and going from call to call and never having enough police officers to be effective, weighed heavily on me.

Another thing that wore on me was the lack of sleep. I never really adjusted to working night shifts because I organized my sleep schedule around being a parent to my four daughters, even if it meant feeling like a zombie. I would maybe catch five hours of sleep a day, with the slightest sound waking me up. I never felt rested.

In July of 2019, I was actually feeling pretty good. But by fall, I began to experience unusual body pains, mostly on my left side. The pains were deep, as if my bones were wasting away. I also noticed my hand would sometimes shake at work, and I felt anxious on police calls that I had done countless times. When I sat in my patrol vehicle to write reports, I looked from side to side to make sure no one would get the jump on me.

Police officers are professional multitaskers—driving at twice the speed limit while getting and responding to updates and planning the next move based on location, distance, and needed resources. It seems like you have to make a thousand small decisions in less than a minute. In addition to multitasking, we also become experts in body language, behavioral cues, and recognizing dangers when no one else does. Unfortunately, like many police officers experience, the skills that keep you alive at work can negatively impact you outside of work. This was the case with me.

I struggled with depression, no longer interested in anything.

In the past, I looked forward to watching college football. That fall, it meant nothing.

When I picked up my girls from school, I always had sunglasses on and constantly checked side to side for dangers. Though there were none,

I felt responsible to stay aware. I started having problems with light sensitivity, frequent headaches, and involuntary weight loss.

By December, I felt sick and weak, with lower back pain and digestive problems, like my body was deteriorating and slowly shutting down. I requested to transfer to swing shift, hoping to get better rest even though it would cost me precious time with my children. Coworkers began asking questions, and all I could say was that I wasn't feeling well.

As I look back now, I realize I hadn't felt like myself for a long time.

I didn't care about anything. My emotional response was zero. If I got a report of a deceased person, homicide, stabbing, or other call where someone's life had ended, I was more concerned about getting the report done and getting some sleep before coming back the next shift to do it again. Also, if I didn't write something down, I couldn't remember it. I felt disconnected from everything. My body stayed on alert 24/7 even when I was home, and I felt mentally frozen in a state of fear as if my life was constantly in immediate danger.

On some shifts, our officers would work all night and then sit in court for most of the next day. They might get a couple hours of sleep if they happened to make it home before their next shift—back to making split-second, life-changing decisions. Even truckers have regulations on how much time they have between shifts. Police officers where I work didn't. I once worked over forty hours straight.

In January of 2020, I left a religious youth group activity I helped lead and began my hour-long commute to work, but my stomach didn't feel right. During the drive, I couldn't catch my breath. My lower back was also in a lot of pain. I pulled over three times, panicking. There were no dangers around. Why couldn't I calm myself?

After the third time, I frantically called into work. When the sergeant picked up, I told him what was happening and let him know I wouldn't be coming in. Then I drove myself to the hospital, thinking I had a kidney stone or something similar. I sat in the waiting room for seven hours—the same kind of waiting room I'd driven many people to who needed help. Worries flooded my mind.

They ran several tests. Everything looked normal. I was told to follow up with my regular doctor. I drove home, but despite the results, I knew something was very wrong. My former self was gone.

Two days after the hospital visit, I met with my doctor. His diagnosis was anxiety. I just wanted something to help me sleep. For the next two weeks, I slept an hour a day at most. I couldn't sit still and spent so much time pacing the house barefoot that my feet became numb. I felt like a lab rat as I tried different medications to help me sleep and be calm.

No matter which medication I tried or how much I took, I'd wake up at 3 a.m. in a pool of sweat—shaking, confused, and terrified. For months, I thought I was dying every day. I would shake, stare out windows, forget where I was, and have other cognitive issues. I could no longer tolerate lights and sounds. I couldn't watch a movie because the depictions moved too fast for my brain to keep up. I'd also get a piercing sound in my left ear, my head repeatedly jerking towards my shoulder as if waiting to hear the next radio update at work. My head and neck throbbed tensely all day long.

Over the course of five months, I lost more than thirty pounds, reaching a weight I hadn't been since seventh grade. My doctor was getting worried. The sensitivity to sound in my left ear increased to the point that if a fork or plate was dropped during dinner, it was like I was hearing the crash of a cymbal, causing me to cover my ears, go into my closet, and cry.

Every two or three weeks, other work-related things triggered crying. I hated it. During these episodes, my children surrounded me and offered comfort while I lay on my bed. At the end of an uncontrollable session of tears, I'd get about five minutes of relief when I felt like myself—until the tingling in the left side of my head started over. This taught me that somewhere inside my mind, I was still okay, and I needed to endure and keep battling to get through this challenge.

I started taking an antidepressant, increasing the dosage as directed. I noted small, positive improvements. At the beginning of the breakdown, I was unable to drive for six weeks because I couldn't focus on the road ahead of me. After being on the medication, I was able to drive again. I also found another medication that helped lessen the intensity of my daily migraines.

In April, after nearly exhausting all my sick and vacation time, and after filing a work-related claim at the suggestion of a friend, I started therapy.

What an amazing blessing!

After a few sessions, I was diagnosed with Post-Traumatic Stress Disorder, directly related to my job in law enforcement. Getting that answer was the best thing that had happened in what felt like forever.

Finally, I had greater insight into everything I'd been struggling with and why. I also began working with a psychiatrist and was diagnosed with General Anxiety Disorder and Major Depressive Disorder. Currently, I'm waiting to find out if my claim for a work-related injury will be approved.

My girls still see their dad cry like a firehose sometimes—then they cry. They've learned not to wave their hands in my face or scare me because of how it triggers me. I'm still on disability and must remind myself all the time that it's okay to not be okay. I've felt incredible shame rocking in a chair all day long while former coworkers have faced Portland riots day after day, their weekends and vacations cancelled. I would have rather stood by them, shoulder to shoulder, than be isolated with a mind I couldn't trust.

I'm no longer married. My former spouse and children have endured vicarious trauma because of me. I live in an apartment away from the place I grew up. When I attend my children's sporting events, I am the guy in the gym startled by the sound of buzzers and whistles.

One might think God isn't prevailing in my life. But I disagree.

I've learned I can endure difficult circumstances and not quit.

I've learned I am much more than any profession, and that relationships in life are what matter most.

I've learned to forgive myself.

I've learned to pray with more intent. When the world isn't right in my head—which is most of the time—I close my eyes and talk with Heavenly Father. When I open them up, I find a few seconds of perfect mind-body connection.

I've learned how to meditate to make the sunshine feel warm and bright again.

I've learned to breathe differently—thanks to yoga on YouTube—which helps my body relax and feel some peace.

I've learned to slow down, pause, and take mental pictures of things to be grateful for.

I've learned the blessing of receiving counseling. I feel gratitude for those who offer their talents to help others in the darkest times of their lives.

I've learned how to support my children's emotional and mental needs during the online school years when they were isolated and unable to be with their peers.

I've learned I have a whole army of people who support me and want me to succeed, even when I feel disconnected and want to avoid them at times.

I could go on and on.

God is prevailing with me.

It's a daily choice whether I will choose Him or not. In choosing to improve myself, I'm choosing *Him*. I've learned to give Him my will.

For a long time, I didn't care if I came home from work or not. But I care now.

I'm learning to trust in God's timing with this mental disease and disorder. I'm in a place where I can accept that this is a challenge for me to work on. I am willing to keep trusting Him because He repeatedly shows me He cares by sending living angels to help exactly when I need them the most. He has always been—and always is—there for me. His work can continue through me if I keep choosing Him.

My body still thinks I'm a police officer at work, responding to stimuli in order to make the right decision to protect myself and others. But my mind is getting better at recognizing, acknowledging, and using the skills I've been taught to bring myself back to reality. I'm learning you don't have to be whole to be healed.

For me, hearing Him is the *process* of being healed—and through this process, He has healed my soul.

"Even if we do not know how to relate to what others are going through, validating that their pain is real can be an important first step in finding understanding and healing."[1]

Reyna I. Aburto

36

My Soul Has Always Known

*"Our true value does not lie in our abilities but
rather in our identity as a child of God."*
Author Unknown

◇◇◇

As a victim of child abuse, I sought safety when I was young by hiding in places to escape the abuse, such as under my bed or within the dark confines of a closet, below the coats and between the boxes. I felt alone, abandoned, orphaned, and trampled on by those who were entrusted to protect me and keep me safe. I felt shame for reasons I couldn't explain, leading to a confusion and numbness that I was "damaged goods."

As I grew older, people told me, "You're a daughter of God. Knowing that should be enough for you to get over your problems." They didn't realize my painful reality.

Victims of child abuse often victimize themselves, feel unworthy of love, and are overwhelmed by the past. Feelings of hopelessness can lead them to hide in a world of illusions in an attempt to escape deep emotional pain.

As a victim of child abuse, I sought to do my ultimate best to try and be good at something—anything really. Yet my terrifyingly violent childhood constantly raised its ugly head, throwing me back to feel in my heart that I was not good enough.

As the years passed, I became exhausted of being that frightened little girl who was overwhelmed by the past. I was tired of hiding in the dark corners of my mind. I was tired of being the victim, fighting for decades against dark, threatening memories and thoughts that were hell-bent on my destruction.

In this process, I desperately prayed to find *someone* who would simply share in who I was. Someone to be excited for me and what I've accomplished. Someone who loved and accepted me completely. I wanted—*needed*—my past to stop holding me captive. I wanted to feel different. I wanted to become a survivor.

In God's time, my prayers were answered, and the Spirit taught me that God really does love me! "There is no fear in love; but perfect love casteth out fear: because fear hath torment" (1 John 4:18).

I was His creation, not a mistake or an accident.

God—the Creator of the universe and all the creations within this vast eternal realm—went to great lengths to create *me*. I was created in His image, with the ability to possess knowledge and feel love. He knows how to help His creations be truly happy and experience joy.

Elder Holland tells us, "The first great truth of all eternity is that God loves us with all of His heart, might, mind, and strength. That love is the foundation stone of eternity, and it should be the foundation stone of our daily life."[2]

I *do* have someone who truly and completely understands my fear, loneliness, anxiety, depression, and pain. I do have someone who shares in who I am. I do have someone who is excited for me and what I've accomplished. And I do have someone who loves and accepts me completely.

It's my Savior, Jesus Christ.

He has suffered more than I can mortally comprehend, and because of Him and His Atonement, I don't need to feel alone. As I've reached out to take His hand, letting Him pull me out of my dark hiding places and into His light, I've begun the journey to escape my victimized prison of childhood abuse.

I am a survivor, and finally my soul whispers what it's always known: "You are a daughter of God!"

"There are times when we have to step into the darkness in faith, confident that God will place solid ground beneath our feet once we do."[1]

Dieter F. Uchtdorf

37

HEALING AND DIRECTION

"I have seen thy tears: behold, I will heal thee."
2 Kings 20:5

◇◇

When my marriage ended in divorce, I went to counseling. During one of the sessions, something from my past came up. I had been sexually abused by someone I trusted when I was six years old. Not understanding what had occurred, I blamed myself, keeping it hidden from others because the perpetrator told me it was "our secret." The pain the abuse caused remained deep inside me, causing me to feel fear and distrust.

It took several more appointments before I was ready to open this area in my heart. When I did, the pain was overwhelming—I wanted to end the session early. Before I left, I assured my concerned counselor we would talk about it next time, telling him I was okay, but inside I was not.

On the way home, old buried emotions overwhelmed me. This time I couldn't push them aside. The next morning, I contacted my counselor, but he couldn't get me in for a week. I was despondent for two days, going through each day feeling heartache and despair. I was like Alma in the Book of Mormon, feeling "racked with . . . torment" (Alma 36:12).

At the end of the second night, feeling weary and tired, I dropped to my knees in tears and cried out to Heavenly Father. My pain was too much to bear, and I pled with Him to take it away. "I cried within my heart: O Jesus, thou Son of God, have mercy on me, who am in the gall of bitterness" (Alma 36:18).

Immediately, the pain was taken from me. It was suddenly gone. My whole body was filled with His love and warmth. He knew what I was going through, and again, like Alma, "I could remember my pains no more. . . . My soul was filled with joy as exceeding as was my pain!" (Alma 36:19–20).

Jesus did this for me. He sacrificed Himself not just for my sins but for the sins and pains that others inflicted upon me. He did this so I could have joy and peace again. Over the next month, I was able to deal with the abuse from my past without the pain I felt weeks earlier.

This healing experience helped me to keep moving forward, strengthening me to make other decisions in which I needed to hear Him after my divorce.

***

Being newly single, I knew I could not support myself on the salary of a medical assistant, so I took a job scheduling surgeries. I thought about going back to school, but I had debt from a degree I had earned earlier that had not been beneficial. I gave the situation a lot of thought, worried about increasing my debt to further my education.

One night, I was praying. I asked the Lord what I should do. I felt a strong impression to return to school to become a physician's assistant (PA). Since I had a bachelor's degree, I felt a master's degree would be the next logical step. I enrolled in a local college and started working on the prerequisites required to enter the program. Because it was a community college, I was able to pay for the classes myself without incurring more debt.

Two years later, I began applying to PA schools and going to interviews. At the end of three years, I hadn't gotten accepted into a program and could not continue paying the costly application fees. I was discouraged. I knew I was directed to take that path, but nothing was coming of it.

I did not accept the setback with grace and patience. I was mad at God. *He* told me to take this path. Didn't He know it would end this way?

I wanted to know why. But no answers came.

My faith began to waver—I was quick to complain.

My dad had given me a plaque I had hanging in my bedroom. It said, "It is what it is—but it will become what you make it." I saw it each night when I went to bed, and it made me angry.

Yes, I can make it what I want—unless God doesn't want it.

I continued going to church each week because it was a habit, but I did not participate in class. I continued to read my scriptures and say my prayers because *they* were habits, but my negative thoughts persisted.

Finally, I talked to my bishop and a friend from church. My friend told me that instead of looking up, I should look at my foundation as a reminder that I could find enough faith to endure this storm. I gave this a lot of thought. I prayed to be forgiven for my behavior and lack of faith. In humility, I asked God, "What should I do next?"

Immediately, I had the thought, *I have always wanted to be a nurse.*

I started researching nursing programs. I discovered the classes I had taken for PA school were the same ones I needed to get into nursing school. I applied to the University of Utah but wasn't selected. I talked to an admission advisor. She gave me ideas to improve my application but told me I couldn't reapply until the following year.

I applied to another school, a private college, and was accepted. Unfortunately, the program was quite expensive. I asked about scholarships, and they were only able to offer a small one. I would need to take out private loans to cover the difference.

Unexpectedly, the university called me back. They decided they wanted me to submit my application for the next semester instead of making me wait a year. Their program cost substantially less than the private college, and they also had more scholarships available. I updated my application for the university, submitted it, and applied for their available scholarships.

Two months passed, and still I had not received a response from the university. The private college needed my answer by the end of the week. I prayed about what to do.

A few days later, I drove to my sister's house, contemplating the decision.

Should I decline the acceptance to the private college, giving up a sure thing for a "maybe"?

Immediately, I was overcome by a warm burning in my chest—I knew what I needed to do. I called the private college and withdrew my application. I said a prayer and told God I was putting all my trust in Him.

Two weeks later, I received an acceptance letter from the university. A month after that, I was notified that I had been offered financial aid—almost a full-ride scholarship.

God had opened so many doors for me to pursue this path. But I wondered why I needed to experience it the way I had when He knew I was to be a nurse.

One Sunday during sacrament meeting, a sister got up and bore her testimony. She shared a story similar to mine, reminding the congregation of a talk given by Elder Holland when he and his son had come to a fork in the road. They did not know which direction to go, and when they prayed about it, they felt they were to go to the left. After a brief time, they came to a dead end. Elder Holland's son was frustrated and asked why they felt it had been the "right path" when God knew it wouldn't go anywhere.

They then turned around and took the road to the right. After driving for over thirty minutes, Elder Holland told his son he was grateful they took the wrong road first. Since it had come to a dead end quickly, they knew they were now on the correct road. If they had taken the right road first, they wouldn't have been sure.[2]

Hearing this made me realize why Heavenly Father had sent me in the direction of PA school. I had thought it was a good choice, but it was not what I was supposed to do moving forward with my life—nursing was. I had no more doubts.

I went to school and earned my bachelor's degree in nursing. I have been a nurse for four years. I love caring for my patients and am grateful for a career I enjoy.

"Be still, my soul: The Lord is on thy side."[1]

Hymn 124

38

My "Mountains"

"If ye have faith as a grain of mustard seed . . .
nothing shall be impossible unto you."
Matthew 17:20

When I think of hearing Him, I know that the further I am from things of this world, and the more focused I am on my Savior's Atonement and keeping the covenants I have made with Him, the more in tune I am with recognizing the whisperings of the Spirit and feeling His love. Of course, this is a work in progress, filled with setbacks and challenges that take a lifetime of effort.

One of the challenges I face is depression.

Hearing Him in the hold of depression isn't easy, but it's possible—through faith.

During my most recent bout with depression, I struggled with not feeling anything except deep, saddening despair. My circuit breaker had flipped, and I was having a very difficult time connecting with my Father in Heaven or recognizing His responses when I prayed. I knew in the back of my mind that all prayers are heard and that those that seek Him are not forgotten, but I was struggling greatly.

It was Sunday and I didn't feel up to forcing myself to go to church. As I contemplated what the day would look like if I didn't, I unexpectedly and faintly felt the love of my Savior. He let me know He was aware of me and that I wasn't alone. This small glimmer of hope, along with the loving concern of my wife, helped me gather enough strength to pull it together and attend church.

Directly after the meetings, we had an appointment with the bishop for tithing settlement. I felt I should share with him what was happening and request he give me a blessing. In the blessing, I was given specific instructions to study the teachings of modern-day prophets. I know this was the Lord's way of showing me where I could find relief from my sorrows and start hearing Him again more clearly.

As I followed the Lord's guidance from the blessing, each successive day brightened a little more. His direction showed the path that led me out of a difficult and discouraging time. Even though initially it felt like my sincere prayers hadn't created a connection to feel Him or receive an immediate response, He was there. He had been listening. Through this experience, I felt a refreshed appreciation of how much the Lord loves me.

My struggles with depression have taught me there is no instant relief, but there is hope in turning to Him. I hold on to faith that He hears our prayers, even if it seems those prayers aren't working.

Like Moroni, I also found comfort in these words: "O Lord, thy righteous will be done, for I know that thou workest unto the children of men according to their faith; For the brother of Jared said unto the mountain Zerin, Remove—and it was removed. And if he had not faith it would not have moved; wherefore thou workest after men have faith" (Ether 12:29–30).

In my life, I am witnessing Him move "mountains" of my own.

PART VIII

Hearing Him When Struggling with Addiction

"He's not waiting for us to be perfect. Perfect people don't need a Savior. He came to save his people in their imperfections. He is the Lord of the living, and the living make mistakes."[1]

Chieko Okazaki

39

Relapse (Almost)

*"The giant in front of you is never bigger
than the God inside of you."*
Author Unknown

◇◇

I had spent the better part of thirty years fighting an addiction to pornography and lust. In my darkest times, I used to visit strip clubs, or "gentlemen's clubs" as they were called. This was the pinnacle of my acting out.

After admitting to myself and others my inability to control my addiction, I finally started to get help. I attended group recovery meetings, asked someone to be my sponsor, learned what my triggers were, and discovered techniques to counter those triggers when they occurred. Most recovering addicts would say that creating a new neural pathway to break the cycle of old habits is one of the hardest things to do when seeking to change.

One afternoon, a few years into my recovery, I was driving down a familiar road in a not-so-good part of town. I knew the area because one of the "clubs" I had visited was there. During the drive, I remembered the club and realized I was close to its location. Immediately I was triggered. It felt like going from zero to ten in milliseconds. I was overwhelmed with desire—no, an overpowering *urge*—to go inside. I could think of nothing else. That one thought consumed me.

Old, well-worn neural pathways took over. I approached the club and pulled into the parking lot. I felt shaky with nervousness, excitement, and fear.

Then another thought occurred to me: "What are you doing?!"

Before I opened the car door, I paused for one second—then another. And in that pause, I heard a voice in my head say, "Call someone."

I had learned in recovery that calling someone before acting out is a way to counter the trigger. I was about to do so, but Satan wasn't going to let me go that easily. My internal battle about whether to go inside the club raged in my heart and soul a few minutes more, which felt like hours. I would reach for the door handle, stop, pick up my phone . . . then put it down again. I repeated this action a few times.

Another thought entered, and briefly I remembered who I was—a son of God. I remembered what I had been through and the recovery I was fighting for.

Slowly, my feelings started to shift. I went from being determined to go inside the club to picking up my phone and calling a trusted confidant to share my situation with. Newer neural pathways were starting to be used—the ones I wanted to strengthen. I picked up my phone. As soon as I started dialing the numbers, I felt relief begin to flow through my body.

The goal of not relapsing that day now felt attainable. I called someone I knew would understand, and as soon as I started talking, I was thankful and relieved, though somewhat embarrassed. I expressed my thoughts out loud and "released" what was happening. The person on the other end of my call completely understood. Without judgement, he loved me and thanked me for calling him.

I had countered Satan's desire to hold me bound to my addiction. I had fought the trigger and expressed my thoughts and desires to someone else, and in that moment, the devil no longer had any hold over me.

Grateful, I started my car and pulled out of the parking lot and back into traffic. With each passing mile taking me farther away from that place, I felt increased peace and thankfulness in my heart.

God had been there.

Hearing Him helped me pause during a critical, impactful, and triggering experience to an addiction I was fighting to recover from. He helped me dial when I was able, then drive away after sharing my dark moment with someone who understood and loved me. Jesus promises "to illuminate the way before us and show us the way out of darkness,"[1] and I experienced that firsthand.

I know He lives. I know He cares for me at all times, loves me in every situation, and is my Savior, Redeemer, and Friend.

"Correct principles enable us to find our way and to stand firm, steadfast, and immovable so we don't lose our balance and fall in the raging latter-day storms of darkness and confusion."[1]

David A. Bednar

40

HE ANSWERED THROUGH SOMEONE ELSE

*"If we repent, mistakes do not disqualify us.
They are part of our progress."[2]*
Dieter F. Uchtdorf

◇◇

It all started in 2016 when I was in the eighth grade.

Curiosity was ultimately the cause of it. I didn't know what I was getting into or the effect it would have on my life. I don't remember where or when I first heard of it, but I can remember the first time I saw it. It seemed to just suck me in.

At first, I could go a couple of days or a week without looking at pornography. But then my desire for it became much stronger, and looking at it every few days ultimately turned into looking every few hours. I didn't want to admit I was addicted.

My greatest fear was my parents finding out about it, so I did my best to keep it hidden. Growing up around technology helped me know when, where, and how to keep things a secret online. For almost two years, the shame it caused drove me to never let anyone know—which of course made it worse—until finally I knew something had to change.

In the course of meeting with my bishop about something else, the Lord softened my heart enough to trust him and share openly what I had been struggling with.

We cried together.

We prayed together.

And as we counseled, my bishop reassured me he could feel my spirit and knew the Lord had great things in store for me. He also told me to remember that the Lord is quick to forgive as long as we trust Him and do our very best. He told me I needed to believe that!

After our conversation, the addiction didn't just go away. I still struggled at times to feel Heavenly Father's love, but my bishop's words kept swirling through my mind. They helped me get through the times when it was still hard, and they were a source of comfort for others as well. Meeting with him was an important step—a tender experience I didn't soon forget.

At the beginning of summer 2018, I was struggling again. I decided to go to a Church youth camp, where we spent time studying the scriptures, learning about our purpose here, and learning how to love others. I had gone to the camp for years previously, but it hadn't made me feel any different. I was still numb to feeling God's love.

On the last day before we were scheduled to go home, a friend pulled me aside to talk. As we walked back toward the dormitories, he said, "I don't know why I feel impressed to tell you this, but I know that no matter how far off the path you think you are, you are never too far away to turn back."

Tears filled my eyes. I knew this statement was the answer to many prayers—from myself, my parents, my Church leaders, and others.

His inspired words that day changed my life.

Soon, after counseling with my parents, I started therapy. There I learned things I use all the time to fight off temptation. Through this experience, I know that God often answers prayers using other people. This is how I have learned to hear Him the most.

"The Son of God perfectly knows and understands, for He has felt and borne our individual burdens."[1]

David A. Bednar

41

HE IS ALWAYS CLOSE

"And how great is His joy in the soul that repenteth!"
Doctrine and Covenants 18:13

◇◇

I remember the discomfort of the cold cement floor, the dark cinder block walls, and the noise. The way I shook, sweated, and experienced tremors, feeling like I was going to die if I didn't get another drink or drug in me.

How could God have allowed this to happen to me?
How could this be His plan? Was He even there?
Did He know who I was? Did He even exist?
How could this be my life?

As a little girl, I loved God and everything related to church. I was the one brave enough to share my testimony with anyone who would listen. I was the girl who gave a Book of Mormon to my fifth grade teacher. I was the girl who wanted people to know that I loved Jesus. I was the girl who knew I was a daughter of God, and I knew He loved me individually and uniquely.

What happened?

My life had become an absolute train wreck. I let worldly doubts creep in and overtake my heart and mind until every day became a constant battle against dark voices—demons in my head telling me I was not good enough and never would be. If God's voice *was* there, I didn't know how to hear Him.

I came to believe that my only hope to get through life was drugs or alcohol—anything that would numb the pain of living in my own skin. I thought I had finally found a "best friend"—the bottle or the drug would never leave me, and I could count on "them" to make me forget the hurt. But using these substances took me on an out-of-control, freakishly fast, spiraling roller coaster. I fell so far and so deep that I didn't care anymore what happened, even if I died.

I was in and out of rehab, in trouble with the law, and in and out of toxic relationships. I lost money, jobs, family, friends, places to live, and my car, burning bridges as I went. I lost everything truly important in life, and as drugs and alcohol took over, I found myself in places I never wanted to be, experiencing things I never wanted to experience. I blamed a mean, angry God who I imagined was looking at me in disgust for how my life had become.

But the truth was that deep down I wanted my innocent life back. I knew there was good inside me, and I desperately wanted to get off the horrible ride, but I had tried and failed so many times that I didn't think it was possible. I made promises when I used, saying this would be "the last time"—I would quit forever and be that good person. Each time I failed, I felt worse—if that was even possible.

After one failed attempt to stay in rehab, I turned to a toxic relationship. I stayed in that relationship for quite some time, questioning if that reality was what my life was supposed to be. One day, feeling so broken and miserable I couldn't handle it anymore, I fell on my knees and tried to pray. I don't know why, and I didn't know if God would be aware of me, but I prayed anyway.

Nothing happened immediately—I was still the girl who thought life was awful and didn't know who God was anymore. But on *His* timetable, things were slowly changing. Miracles were coming.

Not long after, I felt prompted to attend church in the small town where I lived. I met the nicest sister, who I will never forget. She made me feel hope and love again. She talked to me and made me want to find a way out of the life I had been living. Though I didn't realize it at the time, she was the answer to my prayer.

A few weeks later, I knew without a doubt that I needed to leave the relationship I was in. But I was afraid and didn't know how. I reached out to the woman I'd met at church, and she helped me get in contact with the missionaries. The missionaries promptly set up a time for me to receive a priesthood blessing. I was able to leave to get the blessing by acting as if I was going to the grocery store. I don't remember what was said in the blessing, but I will always remember the sense of relief and peace I felt immediately after. The angels God had placed in my path helped me tremendously.

The very next day, God gave me the courage and strength I needed to leave. A twenty-minute opportunity opened up, and God prompted me to take it and go. I had just enough time to pack and leave. It was beautiful—I had heard Him! I knew He loved me and cared about me, and I trusted His timing. I made it safely to my parents' home. I knew God was with me that whole time.

Less than a year passed, and I struggled to stay sober. Things were not going well, and again the demons took over. Soon I found myself back in the scary life of drugs, alcohol, and the same toxic relationship! This time, things got really bad really fast. I quickly got in trouble with the law again and was waking up day after day not knowing where I was, who I was with, or who I had become. Then I found out I was pregnant.

How could God do this to me?

I didn't want it to happen. My life was already a train wreck. It wasn't fair.

But God knew exactly what He was doing.

Maybe I couldn't love *myself* yet, but I decided I was going to do my absolute best to love and care for the baby God was trusting me with. Willingly I made the decision to get sober and turn my life around. God put others in my path to help me.

Unexpectedly, a sweet friend I had known since kindergarten reached out to me. I opened up to her about every detail of my situation. I told her I knew I had to go home to attend court, which gave me a reason to leave the toxic relationship I was in, but I was petrified to face my family and friends. I was also afraid I would relapse again or that something would happen to the baby, so I questioned whether or not to return home. My friend encouraged me to leave immediately—to drive to her house and not even think about looking back. I was scared and wanted to wait a little longer. With her help, I left two days later.

Through this seemingly huge trial, God was there. Facing my family and friends back home ended up being a wonderful thing. My addiction had given me a challenge that God used as a blessing. My baby—an unexpected surprise—ultimately changed the direction of my life for the better.

I am working hard to improve my mental health and maintain sobriety. It hasn't been easy, but it's been worth it. Family, friends, and Church leaders have loved me and helped me. I've learned that God is—and always was—with me, and I can continue to trust Him. During the darkness of my addiction, He was there, just like the scripture says, "Behold, I stand at the door, and knock: if any man hear my voice, and open the door, I will come in to him" (Revelation 3:20).

He was waiting for me to invite Him into my life.

I am so grateful for a loving Heavenly Father who listens to my prayers—both the ones in my heart and the ones I speak out loud.

I know He is *always* close.

"No matter how long we have been off the path or how far away we have wandered, the moment we decide to change, God helps us return."[1]

Dale G. Renlund

42

COURAGE, NOT COMPROMISE

"The Lord sees weaknesses differently than He
does rebellion. . . . When the Lord speaks of
weaknesses, it is always with mercy."²
Richard G. Scott

◇◇

I was born and raised in a household that invited and encouraged gospel participation. My family attended church every Sunday, we had family home evening most weeks, and we read scriptures together on a regular basis. But growing up, my family didn't talk about pornography.

When I was fourteen years old, I flipped through the JCPenney catalog that we received every year around Christmas time. I came across the women's intimate section. I was curious and intrigued by what I saw. This led to a habit of searching the Sunday paper for ads showing women's underwear.

One day, I got the mail and found a Victoria's Secret catalog. The images I saw were provocative and exciting. I took the magazine and hid it in my room. While looking at it alone, I had my first experience with masturbation. I didn't know what was happening. I thought something was wrong with me. Immediately after, I was disgusted by what I had done. The catalog, which moments before had seemed so enticing, became revolting. I felt ashamed and was too afraid to tell anyone what happened. I resolved never to do it again, and I destroyed the catalog.

Despite my good intentions, a seed of curiosity and lust had been planted. Days later, I craved more. The harder I tried to get the thoughts out of my mind, the more they found a way in. The longer I resisted, the more powerful they became.

In the catalog, there had been an advertisement to visit the Victoria's Secret website. One day when I was home alone, I visited the website. I was only there for a few minutes until feelings of shame and guilt persuaded me to turn it off. I was shaking. I knew it was wrong and that God didn't approve.

My thoughts frequently returned to those images.

"The mind is like a stage. During every waking moment the curtain is up. . . . You are responsible for what is allowed on that stage."[3] I felt like no matter how hard I tried, no matter how many times I was successful at denying the adversary access to my stage, he would inevitably gain access sooner or later. And when he did, it didn't take long for me to fall back into the bad habit.

We had annual "porn talks" in priesthood meetings. The general message was "Pornography is bad. Don't look at it. If you are engaged in this, you are not worthy, so stop!" The message I took away was "You aren't worthy. You are weak. You are worthless. There is something wrong with you." I resolved to do better afterward, but eventually I would slip up. The feelings of discouragement and worthlessness that followed grew more unbearable.

I wish I had received counsel on how to handle feelings of curiosity, how to respond to the urges that would arise, how to rely on grace for forgiveness, and how to find strength during the times of greatest temptation. Maybe they were discussed and I just wasn't ready to hear them. Looking back, as a thirty-five-year-old man who has struggled with this for over twenty years, I see my fourteen-year-old self as a boy with a BB gun facing an 800-pound Kodiak bear barreling toward him at 35 mph. However, even in that seemingly helpless state, I knew the Lord was watching over and caring for me.

When I was sixteen, in response to promptings from the Spirit, I mustered the courage to meet with my bishop—a kind, gray-haired man. I thought confessing my sins would be the key to overcoming them. It was a weekday night after youth activities. We went into his office. I fumbled while trying to assemble my words. Finally, through tears I told him about my desire to seek out advertisements for women's underwear. I couldn't tell him about the masturbation—I was too ashamed.

He smiled and told me what I was going through was normal. I could feel the love he had for me. Talking with him helped me understand God knew the struggles I was having, and He loved me! He knew every time I rebelled and every time I gave in despite my best intentions, and still He loved me. He knew every time I successfully resisted and acted with integrity instead of giving into the carnal part of me, and He loved me. He also knew my fight with pornography was far from over. I had a lot more to learn.

After our meeting, I was clean for a couple of months, but over time the thoughts started to creep back—first from stage left, then stage right, then front and center. I was often successful at banishing them, but the more I resisted, the more they returned in strength and frequency. This was confusing to me. Many times I asked in prayer, "Lord, why are these thoughts returning? I don't want them anymore. Don't you want me to be obedient? Why don't you take them away?" I didn't realize I was missing the ingredients I needed for a complete change of heart.

I learned through counseling that, for me, a true change requires four ingredients: conviction, communication, connection, and consecration.

I had conviction—the will to change. And in meeting with my bishop, I had at least started the process of opening the doors to communication. But I was lacking connection and consecration. I needed connection with others who I could trust with my most personal secrets—people I could be vulnerable with, knowing they empathized with me. I also needed a higher and holier cause to consecrate my energy, other than simply "abstinence for the sake of obedience."

For the next two years, I continued to live through the cycle of wanting to change, staying abstinent, relapsing, and falling into despair. It felt like a demoralizing roller coaster.

At eighteen, I left to attend college at Brigham Young University (BYU). This was the perfect environment for me. I was busy and had very little alone time. I shared a dorm room with a roommate and made great friends with those on my floor who were fun, uplifting, and (most importantly for me) almost always present. That environment allowed me to thrive, since most of the triggers at home didn't exist at school. At BYU, I enjoyed two great semesters of abstinence!

By the end of the year, I was preparing to serve a mission. I received my mission call and had two months between the end of the school year and the time I would enter the missionary training center. For those two months, I went home to work and was vulnerable to former triggers. I relapsed a couple of times. Knowing I was preparing to serve a mission helped me quickly get back on track. In my final interview with the stake president, I admitted I had relapsed. Whether by inspiration or compassion, he approved me to serve.

During my mission, there were very few triggers or opportunities to engage in pornography, so it was easy to keep myself clean. I thought I had overcome the addiction for good.

After returning home, old influences flew back into my life. By the time I left for school, I had slipped again.

When I returned to BYU, I was able to stay mostly free from the grips of indulgence thanks to the positive influence of friends, staying busy, attending the temple frequently, and following the counsel of loving priesthood leaders.

During my junior year, a difficult time of struggle returned. As part of the repentance process, my bishop counseled me to stay out of the temple until I stopped acting out on my addiction. I loved the temple, and being told I couldn't go was sobering. Becoming worthy again so I could return became a focused goal. I knew the Lord wanted me in His house, but more importantly, He wanted me there worthily.

Now I had conviction, some communication, and connection, and I was consecrating myself to an end—returning to the temple! With the help of my bishop, I became worthy to attend again. When I returned to the temple, I had one of the most spiritual and uplifting experiences of my life. When I entered, I felt my Savior embracing me with open arms. I knew He had not forsaken me—He was helping me through the process of change.

I met my future wife in the fall of 2010 at a mutual friend's mission farewell. I have no doubt the hand of the Lord was guiding our meeting. I had no intention of being at the farewell and almost walked away once we arrived, but the Lord inspired me to attend. In my patriarchal blessing, I was promised I would have the opportunity to marry a young woman of my choice and would find her as long as I was keeping the commandments of the Lord. I could not have met her if I was not clean from the addiction and able to hear and heed the promptings of the Holy Ghost. She was, and still is, the perfect match for me.

In January 2011, I started my first full-time job for a start-up technology company in Utah. In March, we were married in the Salt Lake Temple. Things were looking up—I had enjoyed over a year of sobriety, and thoughts of pornography were far from my mind. I thought I was on the path to a happy, successful, and easy life!

Shortly before Christmas, my boss told me my job was moving to Washington D.C., and if I wanted to remain with the company, I had to transfer. We had just bought a house, and my wife had over a year left of school. I was not excited to leave, but I had no other job opportunities lined up. After prayer and fasting, we decided I would go. I would find a cheap place to rent while my wife attended her next semester at BYU, then we would sell the house and she would join me in Washington D.C.

The time we were apart was difficult. I lived in a dark, stinky basement apartment with a ceiling too low to stand up in. Work was challenging. I spent a lot of time alone missing my wife. Old triggers returned, leading to me acting out again. Once the semester ended and my wife and I reconnected, things got better.

I thought what we went through was just a result of circumstances. But that wasn't the case.

I traveled a lot for work, sometimes for weeks at a time. This was difficult for both of us, especially after we started having children. This introduced a new trigger. Hotel rooms were hard, especially after long periods of high stress and exhausting travel.

Over the next ten years, my career continued to require me to be out of town a lot. I enjoyed periods of sobriety and suffered times of relapse. Early in our marriage, I admitted to my wife what I was dealing with. While it pained her greatly, she was sympathetic and supportive in my efforts to overcome my addiction. Throughout those years, I also met with priesthood leaders and received guidance and support, building my conviction and community.

In 2020, I slipped further into my addiction than ever before. Behaviors that had only happened when I was away now occurred at home. Thoughts I had dealt with in the past began entering my mind daily. Increasingly I was living a double life. While I tried to limit my access to pornography through filters on my phone and internet, I progressively spent more time finding ways around them.

I discussed with my wife what was happening and met with my bishop. I continued to relapse. A couple of months later, in another discussion with the bishop, he recommended I get counseling through Latter-day Saint Family Services.

My therapist helped me reshape my approach to dealing with my addiction. He directed me to work on forming a community around me that would assist in building conviction and connection by consecrating my efforts on more than just abstinence. This helped me understand that focusing solely on abstinence can ironically lead to more relapses.

This journey has not been easy. It has required me to be brutally honest and vulnerable in ways I never have before. However, through the pains and sorrows I've experienced, I have learned how God sees me—as His son. I understand more clearly that He weeps for me in my struggle but also allows me to wade through so I can grow to be more like Him. Pornography has been a destructive part of my life for many years, and I will need to continue to guard against it for the rest of my life, but I am not weighed down like I once was.

I have shared my experience with many others, including my parents, friends, and fellow Church members. While difficult, through this I have found more community and connection than ever before. I stay open and honest with my wife about my thoughts and challenges, and that has fostered more intimacy and connection than ever before. I am consecrating my efforts to her, my children, and my Father in Heaven.

On the signature line of my email, I have a quote from President Thomas S. Monson: "Courage, not compromise, brings the smile of God's approval."[4] When I first read this, I envisioned someone like Abinadi standing up to King Noah and boldly testifying of the truth despite his pending martyrdom, or Joseph Smith in chains and shackles rebuking the jailers in Richmond, Missouri.

Now I understand it differently as I've applied it to myself.

Now I see a man like me, having the courage to admit he needed help even at the risk of hurting, damaging, or even losing cherished relationships. (And I see a woman who had the courage to forgive even when she felt betrayed.) I see a man who learned to have courage to seek correction even though it's embarrassing and uncomfortable. I see a man who found the courage to get back on the path whenever he faltered, because on the other side of that is a higher and holier place.

Hearing Him has helped me see that He loves me even in my weaknesses. Our relationship with Heavenly Father is the most important thing. Repentance and change is a process, and becoming like Him "requires patience and persistence more than it requires flawlessness"⁵ He is always willing to bring us closer to Him. It takes courage to move closer, especially when it means being vulnerable, but it is worth it!

"God's love is not found in the circumstances of our lives but in His presence in our lives."[1]

Susan H. Porter

43

His Eternal Time Line

"Faith means trust—trust in God's will, trust His way, and trust in His timetable."[2]
Dallin H. Oaks

◇◇

I could tell you a story about how my twenty-five-year-old daughter came to know sobriety and Jesus Christ. I could talk about all that she went through during her five-year battle with severe substance addiction, the destruction that went with it, and what she learned. But as amazing as that story is, it's not mine to tell—it's hers.

As her mother, I will share *my* version of that story—of the nightmare I endured. I can tell about how my faith in God grew through it all and how I learned to hear Him more clearly.

My daughter struggled through high school and grew worse after she graduated. I kept hoping it was not as bad as I thought, but when she fell hard, it went downhill fast. Her life spiraled out of control, and addiction became her escape from the pain. Often I didn't know where she was or if she was even alive. It was heartbreaking. My emotions vacillated. I felt frustrated and helpless. I felt guilty. I felt mad. I felt scared. And I felt very, very sad for her—my precious daughter.

During those years, I heard many loud voices. The voices included my own, telling me I was a terrible parent and that this was my fault.

I heard voices of judgment, real or imagined. I heard voices filled with advice from good people who just didn't know how severe the situation was. It was agonizing. The truth was that I really couldn't help—nobody could—until my daughter wanted to get better.

But there were miracles when I learned to trust the Savior, and in those dark times, I heard Him powerfully yet quietly.

First, He told me He knew my daughter better than I did. He told me He loved her more than I ever could and that He had been helping, teaching, and loving her longer than I had. He told me to be patient with His eternal time line and to believe in His promises. Once I finally started to listen and hold on to faith, I felt peace flowing from Him despite the surrounding darkness. It was strangely wonderful. I had no idea if my daughter would survive, but I knew the Savior loved her infinitely. That message gave me hope and courage to move forward regardless of the earthly outcome.

Second, His reassuring voice subdued my frequent moments of doubt and panic, and His grace soothed my heart many times. During the darkest parts of those years, my husband and I had to draw a very hard line. We could only offer our daughter treatment and rehab because it got to the point where anything else became a source of enabling, keeping her from getting better.

Normally I questioned my decisions and frequently second-guessed myself, but throughout this difficult time, I was given the gift to discern truth. This helped me to follow promptings without looking back and to have the resolve I needed to do hard things without faltering or doubting. When I heard the Spirit, I was able to act with certainty time after time.

Finally, the voice of God taught me that I might never be 100% sure of any outcome in this life, but I could be grateful for any miracle I receive today. It's okay that we're not guaranteed a smooth ride, and it's okay if some prayers aren't answered in mortality. Heavenly Father loves His children, and He will never give up on them. His voice told me His timetable is sacred, and it isn't mine to try to change. His work is eternal. During the scary and uncertain times, He let me know He was working in my daughter's life, and I heard Him tell me, "Today, everything is okay."

To me, the Savior's voice is clearer and more beautiful during our darkest hours because His pure light shines so brightly. I am grateful for the way the darkness of this trial helped me see that light so clearly and feel the depth of His love. "But they that wait upon the Lord shall renew their strength; they shall mount up with wings as eagles; they shall run, and not be weary; and they shall walk, and not faint" (Isaiah 40:31).

PART IX

HEARING HIM THROUGH UPLIFTING MUSIC AND IN NATURE

"Make a joyful noise unto the Lord,
all the earth . . . and rejoice,
and sing praise."

Psalm 98:4

44

SING

"The song of the righteous is a prayer unto me, and it shall be answered with a blessing upon their heads."
Doctrine and Covenants 25:12

Music has always been important to me. There are thoughts and feelings that can only be conveyed through the sounds and rhythm of a well-written song. Even if it isn't church-related, I hear my Father in Heaven through music. I feel His presence when I listen to people share the talents He has given them.

At a low point in our lives, Heavenly Father used music to speak to my daughter and me.

It used to be my job to put my daughter to bed. It was our special time together. As soon as the bedroom door was closed, the rest of the world just wasn't important. I would fight her into her footie pajamas while telling her about my day. She would respond with baby noises. I would lay on the floor and read to her from a board book. She would respond with more baby noises. When we were done reading, I used to wrap her in a blanket and sing to her as I rocked her to sleep. There were several songs, both religious and secular, that we covered every night. When I thought she was asleep, I would sing all three verses of "I Am a Child of God." Then I would stand up as slowly as I could and gently lower her into her crib.

This bedtime routine was the only peace I had while the rest of my life was unraveling. My marriage was crashing down around me. My relationship with God was threadbare. My life was directionless. I had completely lost track of who I was.

I would wake up in the morning, spend the day going through empty motions, and then come home and pretend that everything was fine. It was a whole life made up of muscle memory and conjured happiness. The time I had with my little girl every evening was the only thing that felt real.

A few months before my daughter's third birthday, my marriage ended. It was sudden. One moment we were having a routine fight, and in the next, I found myself homeless, walking around the streets of our small town at 10:30 at night. A week later, I was signing divorce papers while sitting on the front porch of my former home.

I got to go back one more time to put my daughter to bed. As I walked up the stairs to her bedroom, the finality of the situation struck me. This was the last night of normalcy for my daughter and me. I took her into her room and helped her into her pajamas. We skipped the book. I wrapped her up in her blanket and cried as I rocked her. I couldn't sing—I just couldn't get the words out. She fell asleep. I lowered her into her crib for the last time.

A few weeks later, I found a small apartment. My daughter came for her first visit to me, her non-custodial father. She was so happy to see me that she almost jumped out of her mother's arms. But as soon as her mom got in the car and drove away, my little girl panicked. She was inconsolable. I'm sure that in her two-year-old mind, Dad had left her and now Mom was leaving too.

I took her up to my apartment. She wouldn't stop crying. I convinced myself that she hated me. I couldn't make my marriage work, and I felt I had broken my relationship with my daughter as well. She wiggled out of my grasp and sat on the floor against the wall as tears wet her cheeks. I sat on the floor across the room and cried with her. I was alone. My family was broken. I had ruined everything. I was God's one and only mistake.

At that moment, I heard a faint whisper. It was one word—*sing*. I ignored it and continued with my self-loathing. I heard it again. This time, it wasn't just a still small voice. It was a force. I felt warmth throughout my body. I lifted my head and looked at my daughter. I heard the word a third time—*sing*. Through a quivering voice, I began to sing the words to "I Am a Child of God."

The very instant that I started to sing, my daughter stopped crying. She watched me from across the room. As I sang, I felt the truth of the words. *I am a child of God—I'm not a mistake. He loves me. He gave me an earthly home.*

The song became a prayer.

My needs are great. Please tell me what to do. I can learn to do your will, Father.

I put my arms out, inviting my daughter to come sit with me. She stood up and walked over. I embraced her and rocked her back and forth as I sang. Father in Heaven had bonded us while simultaneously reminding me that He loves me. All from just one little song. That's how we stayed until it was time for her to go. We spent her entire first visit sitting on the floor together while I sang all the songs that I used to sing to her at bedtime.

We had found peace together.

"Hymns can lift our spirits, give us courage, and move us to righteous action. They can fill our souls with heavenly thoughts and bring us a spirit of peace."[1]

"Don't demean your worth or denigrate your contribution. Above all, don't abandon your role in the chorus. Why? Because you are unique; you are irreplaceable. The loss of even one voice diminishes every other singer in this great mortal choir of ours."[1]

Jeffrey R. Holland

45

Rescue in a Song

"We can get nearer to the Lord through music than perhaps through any other thing except prayer."[2]
Reuben J. Clark

◇◇

I have heard Him through music, especially when my heart has been filled with anguish, suffering, or loss.

Trauma can live in our cells, leaving a physical imprint on the body as it is stored in somatic memory. Intense emotions at the time of the trauma can initiate long-term responses to reminders of the event.[3] For me, music has been a way of coping with those triggers, helping me feel comfort, release, and peace. Along with hymns, music by Christian artists has inspired me and helped me feel the Spirit again when I'm caught in pain.

One particular time, I was coping with huge upheaval in my life. I was trying to understand the direction God wanted me to go next, and everything felt hard and full of question marks. Each day, I was existing by sheer will, trying to stay calm and continue forward in baby steps, which was all I could handle. I prayed constantly for help in dealing with my out-of-control anxiety. I received promptings to focus on staying in the moment, reminding myself that I was okay for that day.

Several months before, while shopping at Seagull Book, I came across a CD of an artist whose songs I had heard of but didn't know well. I felt like I should buy it, even though it wasn't the type of purchase I usually made there or why I had come to the store in the first place. After I got back to my car, I unwrapped the case and put it with my collection of other CDs in the interior divider of my car door. I eventually played it but not a lot.

Months later, during this time of intense struggle, I was out running errands, fighting tears and loneliness. I felt beaten down by my situation, struggling again with the huge list of raging unknowns in my life. There were so many questions I didn't have the answers to, and I wondered how I could find the strength to keep facing them. I felt broken.

Suddenly, the CD returned to my mind. I found it, brushed the dust off the case, took the disc out, and inserted it into the CD player in the car. Soon music filled the air:

> You are not hidden
> There's never been a moment
> You were forgotten
> You are not hopeless
> Though you have been broken
>
> I hear you whisper underneath your breath
> I hear your SOS, your SOS
>
> I will send out an army to find you
> In the middle of the darkest night
> It's true, I will rescue you
>
> There is no distance
> That cannot be covered
> Over and over
> You're not defenseless
> I'll be your shelter
> I'll be your armor
>
> I hear you whisper underneath your breath
> I hear your SOS, your SOS
> Oh, I will rescue you[4]

As the notes played, one by one my pent-up emotions started to release. Each tear that fell helped lessen a little of the pain, lifting the weariness in my soul. I heard Him through the music. He reminded me He loved me. I was His. He was there. I wasn't alone.

"Inspiring music may fill the soul with heavenly thoughts, move one to righteous action, or speak peace to the soul."[5]

"Worthy music . . . has the power to make us humble, prayerful, and grateful."[1]

Russell M. Nelson

46

BEYOND THE SPOKEN WORD

"Yea, though I walk through the valley of the shadow
of death, I will fear no evil: for thou art with me."
Psalm 23:4

I was stationed at Fort Hood Texas late in 1972 when orders came down reassigning me to Vietnam. My primary job as a chief warrant officer was teaching other pilots how to fly helicopters. I had already served a year in Vietnam back in 1969 and 1970, and I was not excited about the new orders. I went home and told my wife and young son. Christmas was just a few weeks away, and the idea of me going back to the war was not what we had planned.

I moved my family to the West Coast. While in route, we made a stop in Salt Lake City to go to the Church Office Building. I had been called by my priesthood leaders to serve as a Seventy. During the setting apart, I was told to live my life in accordance with gospel principles and all would be well.

I had been to combat before. I knew what I was getting into and how to prepare this time—or so I thought. My leave time went way too fast, much like all leave time does I guess. Before I left, I received priesthood blessings from my father and bishop, said my tearful goodbyes, and boarded the big bird for another tour of combat flying in Vietnam.

When I arrived in Vietnam, I was assigned to the Eighteenth Combat Aviation Company. I was to be their instructor pilot (IP). My job was to check out all aviators in the company and make sure they knew their helicopter and were able to perform their flight duties.

As I performed my IP duties, the days blended into one another. Even Sundays were just another day of flying and teaching. It was hard to teach the new young pilots how to stay alive and perform maneuvers that they had only heard of while being trained back in the States. I flew the new pilots into the jungle and enemy areas to do the missions they were assigned. I helped them learn combat flying—a type of flying only combat can teach. I prayed they would learn it well and maybe—just maybe—survive the awful war.

One day, the flight surgeon told me I had accumulated too many hours and needed a day off. That sounded good to me. The time off fell on a Sunday, so I went to the little makeshift chapel I had spotted a few weeks before. The marquee had three labels: CATHOLIC, PROTESTANT, and MORMON.

I walked in, but no one was there—I was alone. There was a small organ. I played a few hymns I had learned as a young man in my home ward. Then the doors flew open and another soldier came in.

He asked, "Are you a Mormon?"

I replied, "Yep, sure am."

He turned to leave and said, "Be right back." Ten minutes went by. When he returned, he was carrying a box with several three-ring binders inside.

"What are you doing?" I asked.

"I'm leaving to go home in just a few hours, and I prayed someone would be here so I could pass on these records. They're from previous Church members who served here." He dropped the box next to me and left with a handshake.

Since I had nothing else to do, I started reading the records. Some of the notes inside were short, and some were written in great detail. I read about the hurt and loss the members experienced. I read about sacrament talks and testimonies. It was hard. It made me want to be back home with my family and ward members.

Alone with my thoughts and the old church records, I pondered. What was I to do now? I was the only member south of Saigon, Vietnam. How would I get through it?

I made a silent promise and committed that somehow I would maintain contact with the Church and its principles.

***

When the war began winding down, combat units and men were sent back to the States and then home. Because of my ability and experience, I got reassigned to the Joint Military Commission Region VII, specifically the embassy in Saigon. The war continued for me.

My unit was small and we became close. I was still performing IP duties, training men to fly with increased skills and ability. When I flew with them, I shared the gospel whenever they would listen. Some listened, and some would not.

One hot and humid Sunday, I was playing with the automatic direction finder (ADF) radio when all of a sudden, I found myself tuned in to a broadcast of *Music & the Spoken Word* from Salt Lake City, Utah. Every Sunday morning after, I tuned in the ADF and listened to words of wisdom contained in the messages. My weeks then revolved around Sunday and that uplifting message. It was great!

Back home, my family watched the news every evening, often seeing clips of United States helicopters and missions they were flying. This was terrifying for them because they knew it was what I did. They worried and prayed for me all the time.

The war was coming to a close. Peace documents were being signed in Paris. My men and I hoped we would be leaving too—but still not yet. The enemy continued attacking, trying to take as much territory as possible before the cease-fire went into effect. It seemed that my "bird" and crew came under enemy fire every day, but thankfully, the damage was always superficial. No one was hurt while they flew in my helicopter. I was humbled by the priesthood blessings I had received before I left and how my life was being spared.

On a Saturday, I took my crew and flew out toward the border of Cambodia. We were assigned to support a small detachment of Army personnel who were helping to keep the peace. The compound came under heavy enemy fire. Rockets and mortars began to fall all around. One large 122 mm rocket landed in a playground of a school and home for orphaned children. When it exploded, the results were devastating. Dead and wounded children were everywhere.

As we evacuated the wounded and the dead, my heart turned homeward as thoughts of my young son filled my mind. I prayed he would never have to see and experience such a nightmare. Hurt and anger started growing inside me. It wasn't fair—they were little innocent children, not a part of this war. Now they were hurt . . . crying . . . dying.

After we finished the mission, we headed back to base camp. There were bullet holes in the helicopter that needed repairing, a mess inside that needed to be washed out, and lots of reports to write. En route we learned by radio that one of our other helicopters had been hit. There were casualties.

My roommate Anthony was reported dead.

I hated that day! I hated the war! I was starting to develop hatred for everything.

We landed. I gave orders to my crew chief and copilot, turned in my reports, went to my hut, and threw myself on the bed. I sobbed tears of bitterness. I was so angry. It wasn't fair!

I prayed.

Father, where are You?

Why them? Why now?

They were little children! Anthony was my friend!

That night, sleep came fitfully. The anger in my heart was overwhelming.

The next day, we had another mission. I took my crew, and we flew back to the Cambodian border. We were flying resupply missions when the sounds of *Music & the Spoken Word* came over the ADF radio. I was carrying anger and hurt from the day before, and I wasn't interested in listening. But I had made a commitment, so I did.

The message was okay, but it was the closing song that changed my life in that moment and impacted me forever.

> God be with you till we meet again;
> By his counsels guide, uphold you;
> With his sheep securely fold you.
> God be with you till we meet again.
>
> God be with you till we meet again;
> When life's perils thick confound you,
> Put his arms unfailing round you.
> God be with you till we meet again

God be with you till we meet again;
Keep love's banner floating o'er you;
Smite death's threat'ning wave before you.
God be with you till we meet again.

Till we meet, till we meet,
Till we meet at Jesus' feet,
Till we meet, till we meet,
God be with you till we meet again.[2]

That song softened my heart. I felt peace and stillness. My anger and hate were taken away, replaced by the sweet words, "God be with you till we meet again."

"Oh, Father in Heaven," I prayed, "please forgive me. They are with You. With a humble heart and tearful eyes, I say goodbye. I know they are in Your care."

May God be with them till we meet again.

"It is often in the trial of adversity that we learn those most critical lessons that form our character and shape our destiny."[1]

Dieter F. Uchtdorf

47

My Refuge

*"Listen for the voice of the Father in the
bounties and beauties of nature."[2]
Dieter F. Uchtdorf*

◇◇

It was a time in my life when everything familiar was ripped away.
Getting through each day without totally falling apart was often an in-
surmountable task, so I broke it down into minutes.

Breathe—in through my nose, out through my mouth, slowly, deeply, repeat. Focus on now. I was okay—I had what I needed right then.
When my mind scurried frantically ahead into the unknown of tomorrow and I'd start to choke on the reality of my grief, I would start all
over.

Breathe—in through my nose, out through my mouth, slowly, deeply, repeat.

When I wasn't at work, I was alone—in a chilly basement apartment, waiting in limbo for certain things beyond my control to change
before I could move ahead in a new direction. Patience is a hard lesson to
learn when moments, hours, and days seem to drag indefinitely slow and
heart-wrenching pain is lurking at every turn. Sleep was a respite, but
even it was erratic and broken. I wanted a place of temporary relief—no,
I *needed* one.

Spring brought warmer weather and the fresh scent of new budding growth on trees, shrubs, bushes, and grass. The sun lightened my spirit and pushed me outdoors. I had grown up around rugged mountains, dotted with evergreen forests of spruce, hemlock, and white-paper birch. I missed that comfort of home.

One day I was out running errands, and on the return trip back to the apartment, I drove past a park I hadn't noticed before, tucked back a little from the road. When I realized how close it was to where I was living, I decided I would go for a walk there later that evening. After I unpacked the groceries and got a few household things done, I went back, wearing more appropriate footwear.

I parked my car and headed along the path toward the east end of the park. As I walked past some scattered pine trees and a children's playground area, my breath caught. The Wasatch mountains loomed incredibly close. Shades of green filtered through misty light filled my view. As I walked, I felt tension slowly release from my body, rejuvenating my tired muscles and weary heart. The beauty God had created—right in front of me—filled my senses with needed comfort. I felt closer to Him outside in the open air, away from the noise and distraction of the city and crowds. It was easier to hear Him and feel His love.

Over the next several months, walks in that park became my refuge. I received inspiration and guidance while I walked and focused on God. Each time I saw the initial glorious view of the mountains rising up and the uneven skyline of evergreen trees, I experienced peaceful emotions that helped me feel better. "The color green can positively affect thinking, relationships, and physical health. Green is also thought to relieve stress and help heal. Green is calming."[3]

I sensed God in the nearby buzz of bees gathering nectar from clover, sunflowers, and blooms of lavender as they fulfilled their measure of creation. I heard Him in the joyful laughter of children playing, in the cheerful talking of families picnicking, and in the cooling breeze that tousled my hair. When my walks were later in the evening, as the sun was setting, I felt Him in the palette of fiery hues of pink, rose, burgundy, and gold that ran across the sky.

"To truly reverence the Creator, we must appreciate his creations."[4] For "all things denote there is a God; yea even the earth, and all things that are upon the face of it" (Alma 30:44).

"He who notes the fall of a sparrow surely hears the pleadings of our hearts."[1]

Thomas S. Monson

48

The Master Gardener

*"Trust in the Lord with all thine heart; and
lean not unto thine own understanding."
Proverbs 3:5–6*

◇◇

If I ever want to see what the Garden of Eden must have looked
like, I sit on the deck in my mom's backyard for a few minutes. When she bought her home, her backyard was a grassy ex-
panse lined with weeds along the fence. With her talent, time, and
hard work, her space is now an oasis so lush it almost feels tropical.
Of all the traits I inherited from my mother, a green thumb is sadly not
one of them. I once surrendered to her my half-dead ajuga plant, and she
gave it a new home in her front yard. Less than a year later, that ajuga
had tripled in size and was to the point Mom had to prune it back just to
give neighboring plants a little more room.

In September 2020, Salt Lake experienced hurricane-force winds
that toppled some of the oldest trees in surrounding suburbs, their roots
being ripped from the ground. School was canceled, neighborhoods
looked like war zones, and the clean-up took months. In Mom's front
yard, she had a sweet little plum tree that a neighboring tree completely
destroyed when one of its large branches broke off in the storm, snapping
the plum tree in half like a twig.

I remember Mom was sad about her little tree. She used her trusty Sawzall to cut away the offending branch that had crushed it then cut the plum tree at the base. But then she noticed an offshoot of her plum tree that was already a few inches above the dirt. Mom saw that her tree wasn't a total loss. The roots were still intact, and that little offshoot was already growing. So, Mom did what Mom does best. She nurtured that little sprout and grew herself a new tree. When the sprout was taller, she staked it with rope and steel posts to help it grow strong and true. Time passed, and Mom's new tree is now tall and flourishing.

In May 2021, a proverbial hurricane ripped through my life. My oldest son, only seventeen, decided to essentially move out. He suffers from debilitating depression and anxiety. Since he was eight years old, we've tried to help him navigate and manage his disease by trying rehab and therapies, medicines, and different school settings. Any relief he found was temporary. It wasn't long before he decided to self-medicate with drugs and alcohol.

His decision to leave home crushed me.

How are we supposed to do our jobs as parents, care for our son, and keep him safe when he chooses to leave and refuses to come home? The dreams and expectations I had in raising him to adulthood—seeing him get his driver's license, attending school events, meeting his friends, being at his graduation—slid through my fingers like sand in bitter reality.

I was sad.

I was angry.

I was disappointed.

I knew the day in my life would come when my kids would start leaving home. I thought it would be like autumn when leaves gently float away from the trees that have given them a season of nourishment and belonging. Instead, a branch was prematurely ripped from my tree without warning—literally overnight, in one storm.

It hurts.

And it's not like I know exactly where my son is each night. I don't. I pray continuously he'll be watched over and kept safe.

As my heart aches for my son, my spirit aches for peace. I'm grateful I still feel my testimony's strength—it's carried me through some dark times. I know Heavenly Father is aware of our family and our needs. I couldn't have survived this far without His divine help. He sees my storm-ravaged tree and knows I am someone worth saving, even someone beautiful despite the wounds and scarring that come from my life and my trials. I put my trust in Him as He prunes. As I heal and grow under the watchful care of the "Master Gardener," I feel the peace I so desperately want knowing that *He* is also tending my son.

PART X

Hearing Him in Times of Death, Heartache, or Loss

"If you are trying hard and living right and things still seem burdensome and difficult, have courage. Others have experienced these things before you."[1]

Jeffrey R. Holland

49

THY WILL BE DONE

"These things I have spoken unto you,
that in me ye might have peace."
John 16:33

◇◇

Growing up outside of a small town in southern Idaho was, to me, a privilege. The town was small, but the surrounding homesteading and farming community was expansive. Everyone was poor and happy—together.

My chores on our farm sometimes included waiting behind after my father or older brother set the water down the corrugates of the field, making sure nothing blocked it from reaching the bottom before leaving it to run all night. That chore occasionally kept me in the fields until after dark. Many times I had a sibling with me, but just as often, I was alone. The house was not terribly far away—the furthest field about a quarter of a mile away—but a walk in the dark before the brilliant stars appear can conjure up all kinds of scary thoughts.

In time, experiencing this scenario over and over brought me to the understanding that I didn't have to feel alone. I could call upon my Heavenly Father through Jesus Christ to send help to accompany me back home. I realized that I—and only I—had control over whether my walk was in fear or in the peace and solace of the night. It was good practice in hearing Him and feeling His love.

I grew up, went away to college, and married a wonderful young man, and we began our eternal life together. We both had been raised in great families and wanted the same thing in our lives. We were thrilled when we found ourselves expecting our first baby. During those first "grown up" years, my husband and I continued to seek divine guidance through the Holy Spirit as we made some important decisions. We were not left alone.

Nine months came and passed, and our baby still showed no signs she was ready to leave the "nest." Three weeks after my due date, I finally began having real labor contractions. They were sporadic, but progress began. Thirty-six hours later, toward the evening, we were wheeled into delivery. Many new inventions since that time would have been appreciated, like ultrasounds and monitoring.

My doctor determined the baby was not positioned correctly, but he was not able to change that because she was too far down into the birth canal by that time. We didn't have epidurals to help with the pain. It wasn't long before the doctor called for a specialist to help, who arrived soon after.

Together, with a nurse pushing down on each side of my abdomen, they tried everything to complete the delivery. When I heard the specialist tell my doctor that surgery was recommended to save me, I knew we were really in trouble. I had been pushing hard for an hour. His comments increased my determination to deliver our baby.

With all my might, I began pleading with Heavenly Father. *Please don't let my baby die.* After a few minutes, a specific phrase entered my mind that I felt I needed to add: *Thy will be done.*

I knew I needed to add those words, but I wasn't sure I wanted to. Listening to Him can be hard. I continued my pleadings, but this time, I added those four words. As I said them, my spirit became calmer. The more I said them, the more at peace I felt.

Then finally—success! Our baby was born, and I experienced blessed relief. My body, spirit, and soul rejoiced at what had taken place.

I didn't get to see my little daughter before the doctors whisked her away. I was told she was having breathing problems. They took her to get the attention she needed. I believed that everything would be okay, feeling euphoria that I had just partnered with my husband and the Lord in bringing a special soul into mortality. The nurses were sweet and attentive as they cared for me, then wheeled me to a room where I could get some much-needed rest.

I slept.

At about 5 a.m., my husband came into my room and woke me. He told me he and his father had gone to our daughter the night before to give her a priesthood blessing, and my dear father-in-law had suggested they also give her a name for the records of the Church, just in case. I was pleased with the name my husband gave her—our first choice if we had a girl.

He went on to tell me he received a call from the doctor early that morning. The doctor told him that our baby would probably not live.

She passed away before he arrived.

As we sat on the side of the bed and held each other, not quite knowing how to handle this news, it seemed like a warm blanket was suddenly wrapped around both of us. And since we were alone, we knew it hadn't been placed there by earthly hands. It was the first time either of us had experienced the ability and strength of the Holy Ghost to comfort and calm to such an immense degree. Both of us knew in our hearts that our daughter's passing was His will. We came to cherish the fact we had been entrusted with such a special spirit to begin our family.

Because we felt His strength and love so intently, it was a couple of days before I could really cry over our loss. Then the tears flowed on and off for many weeks after.

My testimony of hearing Him, feeling Him, and sharing with Him remains even now, fifty-two years later. As another sign of His love for me, I had another baby one year later on the very same day we lost our first, and then we had five more after that, giving us a family with seven children.

*"He knows of our anguish,
and He is there for us."[1]*

Dallin H. Oaks

50

I Heard a Voice

"We are to seek, in every way we can, to hear Jesus Christ, who speaks to us through the power and ministering of the Holy Ghost."[2]
Russell M. Nelson

◇◇◇

My father was an outdoorsman, and he taught me to appreciate nature. As a young boy, I grew close to him through our adventures of hunting and fishing. He died of cancer when I was fifteen. My world was shattered, and I thought that I would never find anything of meaning again in my life. I really missed my father.

My mother remarried when I was seventeen. I didn't pay much attention, but I know my stepfather didn't try to replace my father. I soon found that they were similar in some ways, like both being hard workers. My stepfather didn't try to push himself on me, and over time he won my heart with his love, concern, and caring. He was always there for me, and over the years, I grew to love him too.

I shared the highs and the lows of my life with him, as well as my aspirations and details about the lives of my wife and children. He always listened and treated my family with the same love, caring, and kindness that he had always shown me. He was truly the best stepfather a young man or young adult could have.

As he and my mother grew older, my mother developed dementia and my stepfather became her caregiver. She could not completely care for herself. He cooked and cleaned and was genuinely concerned about her well-being. However, he also had some health problems and was diagnosed with cancer. It continued to get worse, and he eventually entered the hospital.

As he lay in the hospital near death, I was there by his side. I watched him struggle to breathe, yet he kept holding on to life. As I contemplated giving him a blessing, I heard a voice that said, "Tell him he can go and that your mother will be taken care of." I heard the voice as if somebody was right next to me.

At first, I didn't understand. The voice came again with the exact words. I realized that my stepfather was hanging on to life because he didn't want to leave my mother. He was the caregiver to the end. I understood that he needed permission to move on and the reassurance that my mother would be taken care of.

I gave him a blessing and followed the instructions that I was given. I told him he could go, he could pass on, and that my mother would be taken care of. Shortly after the blessing, my stepfather took a deep breath and passed away peacefully. I was so thankful for the voice of the Lord, that I was able to hear Him, and that He gave me the instruction I needed in that moment. I was so blessed to have both a wonderful father and the best stepfather I could've asked for.

"When you feel like you are drowning in life, don't worry— your Lifeguard walks on water."

Author Unknown

51

Searching for Peace

*"Be of good comfort . . . and the God
of love and peace shall be with you."*
2 Corinthians 13:11

My whole world fell apart four years ago when my fourteen-year-old son took his own life. He hanged himself in his bedroom in the middle of the night. Until that moment, I used to be comforted knowing my kids were home for the night and safe in their rooms. His death threw me into an incomprehensible new reality. For a long time after, my brain tried to convince me I was in an ongoing nightmare I needed to wake up from.

He was my middle child, with three older siblings and three younger. He had a close and connected relationship with all of us, always trying to help us laugh and be happy. His death was extra shocking because the year before, we believed he had made it through his struggle with severe depression and anxiety. He had seemed much better. Then suddenly he was gone.

Our family came to a crushing halt. Because we didn't know how to handle our emotions or navigate life anymore, severe depression reigned in our home. Eventually, I found sources and coaches able to help me figure out how to process my feelings better and work through my grief. With time, I improved a lot but still had areas of struggle.

I remember listening to a television show where two people were discussing grief. One asked the other how to know if he had made it through the grieving process. His friend suggested he would know if, when he looked back, he felt a sense of peace over his loss. I wondered if feeling peace over my son's death would ever occur for me.

My husband and one of my children suffered greatly over my son's death, trying to figure out how to become functional again. As I tried desperately to work through my own issues, I felt responsible for helping each member of my family make it through *their* emotional struggles as well. Taking on their pain made me think I could never feel better until all of them did.

I listened to a book on the power of finding peace in our lives. The book taught that as you let go of the pain of those around you and find your *own* peace, that peace will radiate from you and help others find it as well. This impressed me and created a distinct shift.

God was looking out for me, helping me find sources to understand the peace He offers and how to obtain it for myself. He used the Spirit and other people to guide me to the teachings He knew could help me the most. For me, this was hearing Him. He promises, "Peace I leave with you, my peace I give unto you: not as the world giveth, give I unto you. Let not your heart be troubled, neither let it be afraid" (John 14:27).

It's been an emotional journey, but as I've let go of the pain of those around me and concentrated on my own healing, I have been blessed with greater peace. I have also seen all of my family make great progress, working through their grief and finding peace of their own.

"That which is taken away from those who love the Lord will be added unto them in His own way. . . . The faithful will know that every tear today will eventually be returned a hundredfold with tears of rejoicing and gratitude."[1]

Joseph B. Wirthlin

52

I Closed My Eyes and Opened My Heart

*"And thou . . . shalt shew them
the way wherein they must walk."
Exodus 18:20*

◇◇

My wife was dying of a rare, aggressive form of cancer, and I couldn't continue to work and be her full-time caregiver at the same time. I knew caring for her myself was what God wanted me to do, even though it raised a lot of questions and uncertainties about the future. For financial reasons, we decided we had to sell our house and move—we just weren't sure how to go about it or where we would go after. I had been praying for weeks for direction and answers.

One day, I sat on the front lawn with a good friend talking, listening to the cars go by, and looking at the flower garden I had spent many early-morning hours weeding. His wife was inside the house with my wife, giving me a brief respite. I explained to him my frustration of not knowing what to do. He had recently been released as stake president. He shared with me his experience and gave some advice.

He referenced a time in his own life when he was thinking about taking a new job. It included a long-distance move, and he had felt feelings of frustration over his seemingly unanswered prayers regarding what he should do. Finally, he felt the answer was to make a decision and proceed forward until the Lord put a roadblock or barrier in his way. His words gave me a warm, peaceful, tingly sensation from my head to my feet. I recognized it as truth coming from Spirit. I decided to talk to my wife about his counsel. To me, it felt right.

After talking to her and hearing her agreement, we decided we would pursue the path of listing our home as "for sale by owner" and see where the road took us. It was scary to think we didn't know exactly where we would go if the house sold quickly. There were many factors that played into a decision of where to move, including proximity to our doctors, hospital, and clinics; my wife's need for comfort and privacy; and our pets. But we are promised that "faith always defeats fear."[2]

Over the next several weeks, as I prepared the house to get ready for sale, I had calm feelings that the Lord was aware of us and our situation. Having a direction felt right, but we were vigilant in looking for any barriers the Lord might place in our path. Once my preparations were complete, I listed our home for sale on several free websites.

Questions continued to fill our minds, and we took them to Heavenly Father in prayer.

Where do we move once the house is sold? Do we buy a less expensive mobile home for cash? Do we rent something? Do we live with friends or relatives?

No answers came.

We had to make decisions and trust that if it was not the Lord's will, He would put a barrier in our way. So, onward we went, but nothing was coming together as we pursued several options.

Around this time, we had a professional estate sale company spend two long weekends preparing and directing the sale of most of our possessions. We knew we wouldn't be able to keep 95% of what we owned. That loss was hard, but it was a sacrifice we knew we needed to make. It was especially difficult for my wife. She was dying, struggling to find some sense of comfort and peace in that new reality, while everything familiar around her was being taken away.

During the sale, we met Dan.

He came by early one morning to buy a bunch of my larger woodworking tools. He was a farmer who lived about an hour north of us. He told us he had a small corner in one of his fields where a person could park a recreational vehicle (RV); hook up to power, water, and a septic system; and live there.

My parents had an older, forty-foot motor home. I talked with them, and they agreed they would sell it to us if we wanted. I talked with Dan again. He told us we could park the motor home on his land, and with just a few site improvements, we'd be able to stay there without any rent for as long as we needed.

This felt like the answer!

We could now start to focus on the RV, arrange contractors to do the site improvements, and move. This would keep us close enough to the doctors and clinics we needed to visit for my wife's care, and it would also give us privacy and peace in the country.

Within a few days of deciding this, we signed the contract for the sale of the house, with enough equity to fund the purchase of the RV and make the needed site improvements. There seemed to be no barriers. We felt excited, thinking we were heading in the right direction.

As inspections and appraisals materialized, we realized we would have a few weeks where we would need to stay with someone while we bought the RV and did the site improvements. A friend of mine who was a recent widower generously agreed he would let us stay with him for a while. The plan was all coming together.

During this time, my wife's illness had progressed and her health significantly declined. When surgeons attempted to remove the tumors in her original surgery, they found the cancer had metastasized, spreading to nearby organs. This made the surgery more complicated and invasive, and it didn't produce optimal results. Because of this, my wife had a recurring infection at the surgery sight. It would heal just enough to close the wound, then within a short time it would reopen, filled with new infection. Her doctors weren't able to determine its cause or successfully keep it from coming back. She was in a lot of pain and had become mostly immobile. However, there were still no significant barriers stopping us from moving forward with our housing plan.

A few days before we were supposed to move from the house, we had been to a doctor's appointment where they tested the blood and drainage from my wife's open wound. The morning before we were supposed to move in with my widower friend, we got a call from the doctor's office with the results. They were not good.

My wife had two serious infections—staphylococcus (staph) and extended-spectrum beta-lactamases (ESBL) Escherichia coli—both of which are highly infectious and very difficult to treat. This was the barrier God was placing in our path—the roadblock setting us on a different course.

With the highly contagious infections, we weren't able to stay with my friend due to a recent medical condition of his. This was the same reason we were not able to use our backup plan, which was to stay with my elderly parents, because they also had existing medical conditions.

Questions and concerns filled my mind.

How was I supposed to care for my sick and dying wife? Where would we go, and what would we do? Did I have enough faith to continue?

The months of planning and preparation seemed to be for nothing.

It felt like a "Peter" moment. Did I have faith similar to Peter—to take a step outside of the boat amidst the storm and walk on the water toward Christ?

Once again, I closed my eyes, opened my heart, and talked with God. I slowed my breathing and let Him take over. I knew that whatever was next was His plan now, so I trusted in Him and it. Soon I felt I should make a few phone calls, first to my bishop and then to family to let them know what was happening. I made the calls. Then I was still. God had this.

Miraculously, within a few hours, our path shifted direction. God had been preparing two different families to help us. Both of them contacted us and offered us a place to live so I could continue to care for my wife for however long she had left.

After discussions with each family, we chose one. They were a family of seven who offered their master suite with a private bath and one additional room. They rearranged their entire family's living situation to accommodate us, including our dog and cat. They were healthy and undaunted by the potential spreadable infection. We were beyond grateful and moved in.

Within a few months, that family's situation changed and they were moving. Once again, the Lord provided us accommodation with another couple in our ward who generously came forward and opened their home to us as they listened to the Spirit. Many lives were touched and blessed by the generosity of those who helped us.

We heard Him as we simply kept moving forward in faith, trusting that if the direction we headed wasn't what He wanted, He would put a barrier in the way. And when He did, we knew we would then have to follow His lead to direct our path.

Several months later, my wife passed away.

Through this experience, I learned how to be better at listening to God, how to more trustingly follow Him, and how to more readily act in faith, even when I didn't know where the path would go.

"We need to decide which among all the different voices we will obey. Will we follow the unreliable voices advocated by the world, or will we do the work required to allow our Father's voice to guide us in our decisions? The more diligently we seek His voice, the easier it becomes to hear. It's not that His voice gets louder but that our ability to hear it has increased."[1]

David P. Homer

53

HE CAUGHT MY ATTENTION

*"The voice of the Lord came to them in their afflictions,
saying: Lift up your heads and be of good comfort . . .
and I will also ease the burdens which are
put upon your shoulders."*
Mosiah 24:13–14

There are some events that happen in your life that you will always re-member—the date, time, sights, smells, and feelings. For me, that came twenty-two years ago when I was diagnosed with breast cancer at age forty-six.

I had gone in for my regular mammogram appointment. Since I hadn't heard anything back, I assumed all was well. Then one day, I received a call from my doctor asking me if I had picked out a surgeon for my surgery.

What surgery?

Next thing I knew, I was scheduled for a biopsy and CT scan. Then I was waiting for answers.

On the Friday before Memorial Day weekend, I was anxious. My physician was going out of town, and if I didn't hear anything that day, it would be a very long three-day weekend. My husband and twins were

291

out doing their paper route, and my oldest daughter was watching television in the family room when the phone finally rang.

It was the radiologist with my results. His first words were, "I'm so sorry, but you have breast cancer. Let's get this taken care of." After we finished the conversation, my emotions overwhelmed me. I threw the phone down and started to cry.

I lived down the street from my parents. Knowing they were home watching the news, I quickly left my house. I ran down the street, burst through their front door, raced down the hallway to the family room, and threw myself in my dad's lap. I was crying so hard I couldn't talk.

Quietly my mom said, "You have cancer, don't you?"

"Yes," I blurted. Then I added, "I'm scared . . . and worried."

My dad was gently stroking my head, trying his best to comfort me. My mom knelt down on the floor beside me, hugged me, and said, "It's going to be okay."

My feelings and thoughts were in turmoil.

Two days later, in sacrament meeting, we were sitting next to my parents like usual. During the meeting, my dad passed me a note that said, "I am completely convinced that you are going to be all right and that the Lord will heal you."

Well, *I* wasn't convinced.

For the next few days, I went through a whole range of emotions, one being anger. I spent a lot of time in my backyard weeding and edging while I tried to process this diagnosis. At one point, while kneeling in front of some rose bushes to pull out an overgrown morning glory plant, I began to pray. I was almost yelling at my Heavenly Father.

"Why me?! I'm trying to provide for my family. I have a daughter getting married in a few weeks, and I have so much to do. I don't have time for this! Do you hate me?" Tears rolled down my face. So overwhelmed by emotion, I almost missed hearing a small, gentle whisper.

"My daughter, I love you."

He had caught my attention.

He said again, "I do love you—and why *not* you? Do you think I'm doing this to punish you? I'm not. There are lessons for you and others to learn from this experience. I'm offering you an opportunity to learn and grow."

A sweet, calm, and peaceful feeling came over me. My next prayer was filled with gratitude. I am forever thankful for that special moment that was given to me to hear Him.

My cancer journey was not easy. I had surgery on June 6 and started radiation therapy on July 6. I went to radiation therapy five days a week for six weeks. My skin is very fair, and I burned within the first week. I spent considerable time reading my scriptures and trying to learn what Heavenly Father wanted me to. I did experience growth, and I felt His watchful care and healing power bless my life. After I was declared cancer-free, I recorded that part of my journey in a special journal dedicated to my family and Him.

"For after much tribulation come the blessings. Wherefore the day cometh that ye shall be crowned with much glory; the hour is not yet, but is nigh at hand" (Doctrine and Covenants 58:4). What comfort to know that there are blessings from tribulation and that working through the challenges will bring us glory!

"The Savior loves to restore what you cannot restore; He loves to heal wounds you cannot heal; He loves to fix what has been irreparably broken; He compensates for any unfairness inflicted on you; and He loves to permanently mend even shattered hearts."[1]

Dale G. Renlund

54

LISTENING THROUGH MY EARS, EYES, MIND, AND HEART

"Faith cometh by hearing, and
hearing by the word of God."
Romans 10:17

I had applied to numerous graduate programs and was waiting to see if I had been accepted. During this time, a friend asked if I was interested in going on a blind date with her and her boyfriend's roommate. I decided it wouldn't hurt anything, but I was not expecting fireworks. I was content in my career, and my focus was on graduate school.

My husband-to-be came to the door wearing a ball cap backward. Later I learned this was to hide his baldness. I thought he was cute and attractive. He was funny, and we seemed to have a connection. He had found out my favorite candy was sour apple Jolly Ranchers, and he had hand-picked them out for me. It was a simple gesture to show he was thinking of me, and it won me over.

We dated for six months and were engaged for eight. Lots of prayers went to heaven to make sure marrying him was the direction I was supposed to take in my life. There was no thunder or earth-shattering answer—just simple calmness and peace. I learned this was hearing Him.

We were married in the Salt Lake Temple in October 2006. It was a great honor to be married in the same temple as my parents and grandparents. When I looked at my sweet family and friends in attendance, tears fell down my face. I was grateful for the quiet simplicity of love. This opportunity and remembrance of that day, and the covenants and promises made between my husband and I, gave me strength later . . . to hold on.

My husband and I felt that since we were "older" when we got married, we shouldn't wait to start having a family. Motherhood was extremely important to me. When I was little and people asked what I wanted to be when I grew up, my answer—given with strength and conviction—was always, "A mom!"

Doctor visits, fertility treatments, and agonizing financial situations brought tears of frustration for the next three long years. To me, it felt like a lifetime. I felt spiritually drained—exhausted. I was doing my part, so why wasn't it happening for us?

One day, while kneeling by my bed, I laid out my heart and had a soulful conversation with my Father in Heaven. I let Him know I understood this trial was shaping me and who I would become, but it was hard! I felt a strong urging from the Spirit that it had to do with timing and that I needed to trust in Him.

Dieter F. Uchtdorf explained, "At times we may feel insignificant, invisible, alone, or forgotten. But always remember—you matter to Him!"[2] I felt peace within my heart. One way or another, in His time, I would become a mom eventually.

In December 2009, I was at the State Capitol Building listening to my special needs clients sing in their annual Christmas choir. I saw their smiling faces, felt the warmth of their excitement, and loved listening to them sing their hearts out. It was a magical experience. A special kind of love filled the room that day, and I got teary-eyed. Suddenly, my phone was vibrating. It was the doctor's office. I quietly got up, slipped to the back of the building, and took the call.

The nurse on the other end told me my test had come back positive. I started crying tears of happiness for the long-awaited dream. I felt like the thick door that had been stuck between me and motherhood had finally opened, allowing me walk through and move to the other side. My emotions were all over the place. I fact-checked about four or five times. "Are you sure? Are you sure?" I asked over and over.

She could hear me crying. She knew about my long wait. "Yes. We are so excited for you!" she replied.

A friend who was nearby, who I had shared my fertility struggles with, saw my tears. "Are you okay?" she asked. "Do you need anything?

I could see she was concerned. "I'm fine," I reassured her. "These are joyful tears."

I held on to my pregnancy news as a sacred experience. It felt fragile, like I needed to protect it and tuck it safely into my heart. Looking back, I know the reason was that I needed to savor every moment of the pregnancy and simply let it be.

After the phone call, I excused myself and went into the parking lot. In my car, I offered a simple but heartfelt prayer of gratitude to God, expressing that I knew this was a tender blessing and recognized His hands in bringing it into reality.

We soon learned other complications were occurring with this pregnancy, including issues with the placenta. Driving at midnight to the closest emergency room to make sure everything was okay added more financial debt and worry. There were five more trips to the ER. The medical professionals kept telling my husband and I that if I could make it to twenty-eight weeks, we were doing well. With each subsequent ER visit, I held my breath with hope until they found our baby's heartbeat. Once it was detected, I felt my own heart could beat again.

June 24, 2010, started out as a beautiful bright day full of sunshine with ninety-eight-degree temperatures at 9 a.m. I received a call while at a home visit that one of my clients was having a medical emergency. The family asked me to come meet them at the hospital. I let them know I was on my way.

In my car, I buckled my seat belt, preparing myself mentally to meet them and offer my assistance. While driving northbound, I saw something concerning.

What is that guy doing?

A car was headed in the wrong direction.

I was in the furthest lane on my side, and there was no way to get over any further. The oncoming car hit me head-on.

Everything went black.

When I woke up, I saw my windshield broken into tiny shards of glass. In the reflecting sunlight, there were little rainbows all around me. I felt the Spirit tell me to stay calm. I softly closed my eyes and said a prayer for help. I asked for calmness and comfort. I was feeling alone. The next thing I heard was the creaking of the back passenger door. I couldn't see who it was. My legs were trapped under the engine of the car. I couldn't move.

A reassuring male voice spoke. "Hi, I'm Brian and I'm an off-duty paramedic firefighter. I live across the street. I heard the accident and came to help you. I'm going to hold your neck—please try not to move. We need to keep you as straight as possible." Brian then started asking me a series of questions: "What's your favorite color? What's your favorite food? Favorite dessert?"

Later I learned these questions were saving my life. He was doing his best to keep me conscious while the first responders were on the way.

I was trapped in my car for an hour and a half. The firewall of my car that holds the engine dropped on my lap—I was immobilized. During the time they worked to release me, in ninety-eight-degree temperatures, the fire chief became concerned that his team of paramedics and fire-fighters were going to suffer heat exhaustion. I distinctly heard a fire-fighter say, "Chief, please don't call in another unit. I feel like we need to stay with her and save her."

The trauma unit from the hospital also sent me an angel in dis-guise—Nurse Debi. She came into the car through the back and crawled over the seats.

I told her, "I'm pregnant. Please save my baby."

She put the Doppler on my tummy to listen to the heartbeat of the baby. She smiled. "Honey, it's really loud in here because they're using all of the machines to try to extricate you. I'll wait and check again when you're out." She provided me with much-needed maternal comfort.

As soon as she left the car, I knew—my sweet baby was gone. My baby had died. The baby I longed for, prayed for, and fasted for. My dream of being a mom was gone—through no fault of my own.

I was placed in a medically induced coma for a week as my body endured orthopedic surgeries, skin grafts, and several other extensive surgeries to help my wounds heal—wounds that my body physically sur-vived. However, the physical pain I endured was nothing compared to the emotional distress and heartbreak of having my daughter, Livi, die.

Since I couldn't move, I spent hours in bed praying, meditating, and soul-searching. Familiar tunes, Church hymns, and uplifting songs provided relief and solace when my pain medication no longer worked. A dear friend sent me this message: "The Lord compensates the faithful for every loss. . . . Every tear today will eventually be returned a hundredfold with tears of rejoicing and gratitude."[3]

***

The Chinese character for listening is made up of four different elements—ears, eyes, mind, and heart. We use our *ears* to listen and pay attention to not just spoken words but also to another's relationship to those words. We use our *eyes* to connect with the person we are listening to by giving them our attention and gaining insight into their thoughts. We use our *mind* to consider the words and ideas shared. And we use our *heart* as we empathize with the person we're listening to, experience the emotions they share, and feel compassion for them.[4]

I experienced these elements as I learned to hear Him more completely during this heart-wrenching, soul-searching time. I learned how to help myself and to be more aware of how to help others.

I heard Him with my eyes.

I saw how much Heavenly Father really did love me. He sent me a daughter that I carried until thirty-two and a half weeks, and she saved my life. The fire chief reported I would have died on impact, but because I was pregnant and so far along, my baby provided me with extra protection to all my vital organs.

I saw little miracles along the way, including the fact that the off-duty paramedic firefighter lived across the street from where my accident occurred. I saw with my eyes the first responders who didn't leave until I was extracted. And I heard Him through seeing Nurse Debi, who came to me, held my hand, and told me it would be okay. Her presence was like a warm blanket wrapping me in love.

I heard Him through my mind.

In my prayers and fasting, I learned I have to be open to allow Heavenly Father to be at the helm of the ship—to believe in Him always and to know we are here to strengthen our ties with Him and with heaven.

I heard Him through my heart.

I learned that going through trials is hard. Life is hard. We might not get the answers to our prayers that we believe we need, but He will carve a way in our life to mold our hearts into what they need to become. I learned to reach out and help others, changing my life and theirs.

Heartfelt acts of kindness bring me closer to my Heavenly Father and my little Livi.

We all can listen better—with our ears, eyes, hearts, and minds, with undivided attention. And we can help others hear Him through us as we serve like He would.

CONCLUSION

From the Authors

"Joy does not simply happen to us. We have to choose joy and keep choosing it every day."[1]

Henri Nouwen

55

CHOOSE JOY

*"Wherefore, be of good cheer, and do not fear, for I the
Lord am with you, and will stand by you."
Doctrine and Covenants 68:6*

There are times in life's journey when something is said and heard many times, but until it's *truly* heard and understood, it just floats around the conscious mind, often hanging in the sidelines of jumbled thoughts and random trivia. And then, when that true moment of impact occurs when hearing Him, the meaning and message it sends becomes clear and personal and can create lasting change.

We experienced this in the spring of 2020 during a particularly difficult, course-altering event. Life felt dismal and dark. As we turned to God for help, His light shone through. "He that receiveth light, and continueth in God, receiveth more light; and that light groweth brighter and brighter until the perfect day" (Doctrine and Covenants 50:24).

In the darkness, God reminded us that even though He knew and understood all the hard things we had gone through, suffered, and felt, we still had a choice. We could still focus on all the good parts of our lives, and we could still choose joy despite our difficulties. As our focus shifted to realize how much control we actually had by changing our thoughts and perceptions—something we had heard many times before—we became different. We had many things to be grateful for, and as we made an effort to take notice of them (even the small things), our lives were better and *we* were better.

"We can choose to be grateful no matter what. When we are grateful to God in our circumstances, we can experience gentle peace in the midst of tribulation. In grief, we can still lift up our hearts in praise. In pain, we can glory in Christ's Atonement. In the cold of bitter sorrow, we can experience the closeness and warmth of heaven's embrace."[1]

So, we *can* talk about broken relationships and broken families. We can talk about depression and anxiety, heartache, abuse, addiction, suicide, and betrayal. We can talk about fear, loneliness, loss, and death. We can talk about wanting to give up, being rejected and misunderstood, being judged unfairly, and facing overwhelming tiredness and sadness. We have experienced them all.

But we can *also* talk about love, compassion, empathy, kindness, healing, and forgiveness. We can talk about strength, peace, gratitude, and grace. We can talk about trust, endurance, recovery, faith, unity, and connection. We can talk about new beginnings and the value and wisdom of letting a painful past go to be more fully in the present. We have experienced these as well.

We've learned that focusing on the latter—choosing joy, focusing on Him, and listening to hear Him—lifts our hearts and lightens our souls.

"If we approach adversities wisely, our hardest times can be times of greatest growth, which in turn can lead toward times of greatest happiness. . . . If we do our part, He will step in. He who descended below all things will come to our aid. He will comfort and uphold us. He will strengthen us in our weakness and fortify us in our distress. He will make weak things become strong."[2]

—Diony and Trent

How Can We Hear the Father's Voice?

"As you pray to Him in the name of Christ, He will answer you. He speaks to us everywhere.

As you read God's word recorded in the scriptures, listen for His voice.

During general conference and later as you study, listen for His voice.

As you visit the temple and attend church meetings, listen for His voice.

Listen for the voice of the Father in the bounties and beauties of nature, in the gentle whisperings of the Spirit.

In your daily interactions with others, in the words of a hymn, in the laughter of a child, listen for His voice.

If you listen for the voice of the Father, He will lead you on a course that will allow you to experience the pure love of Christ."[3]

NOTES

Introduction: Learn to Hear Him

[1] Russell M. Nelson, in "President Nelson Shares Message of Hope during Coronavirus Outbreak" (address given Mar. 14, 2020), newsroom. ChurchofJesusChrist.org.

[2] Russell M. Nelson, "Hear Him," *Ensign* or *Liahona*, May 2020, 89.

[3] Spencer W. Kimball, "Revelation: The Word of the Lord to His Prophets," *Ensign*, May 1977, 78.

[4] Boyd K. Packer, "The Candle of The Lord," *Ensign*, January 1983, 52–53.

[5] *Teachings of the Prophet Joseph Smith*, sel. Joseph Fielding Smith (1976), 151.

[6] Dieter F. Uchtdorf, "Receiving A Testimony of Light and Truth," *Ensign* or *Liahona*, Nov. 2014, 21.

[7] *A Story to Tell* (Salt Lake City: Deseret Book, 1945), 320.

[8] Russell M. Nelson, "Hear Him," 90.

[9] Russell M. Nelson, "Hear Him," 90.

[10] Henry B. Eyring. "The Reward of Enduring Well," *Ensign*, July 2017, 4.

1 I Love You

[1] Henry B. Eyring, "The Holy Ghost as Your Companion," *Ensign*, Nov. 2015.

[2] Susan H. Porter, "God's Love: The Most Joyous to the Soul," *Liahona*, Nov. 2021, 33.

2 He Laid It Out in My Mind

[1] Brent H. Nielson, "Is There No Balm in Gilead?," *Liahona*, Nov. 2021, 58.

3 Where Did I Feel Peace?

[1] Elder Ciro Schmeil, "Faith to Act and Become," *Liahona*, Nov. 2021, 31.

4 A Light unto My Path

[1] Ronald A. Rasband, "Behold! I am a God of Miracles," *Liahona*, May 2021, 111.

[2] David A. Bednar, "Watchful unto Prayer Continually," *Ensign* or *Liahona*, Nov. 2019, 34.

[3] "Joseph Smith's First Prayer," *Hymns*, no. 26.

5 In the Valleys of Our Lives

[1] Walter F. Gonzalez, "The Savior's Touch," *Ensign* or *Liahona*, Nov. 2019, 92.

[2] "Nephi's Courage," Children's Songbook, 120–21.

[3] Russell M. Nelson, "Hear Him," *Ensign* or *Liahona*, May 2020, 89.

[4] Richard G. Scott, "Learning to Recognize Answers to Prayer," *Ensign*, Nov. 1989, 32.

6 Answered Prayers—LGBTQ+

[1] David B. Haight, "Personal Temple Worship," *Ensign*, May 1993, 24.

7 He Answered Immediately

[1] Michelle D. Craig "Spiritual Capacity," *Ensign* or *Liahona*, Nov. 2019, 19.

[2] Dieter F. Uchtdorf, "The Merciful Obtain Mercy," *Ensign* or *Liahona*, May 2012, 77.

[3] Dieter F. Uchtdorf, "The Merciful Obtain Mercy," 75.

Part II: Hearing Him through the Holy Ghost

[1] David A. Bednar, The Spirit of Revelation," *Ensign* or *Liahona*, May 2011, 88.

10 Whisperings through the Spirit

[1] "Let the Holy Spirit Guide," *Hymns*, no. 143.

[2] Dieter F. Uchtdorf, "The Love of God," *Ensign* or *Liahona*, Nov. 2009, 23.

12 He Loved Me for Who I Was

[1] Joy D. Jones, "Value Beyond Measure," *Ensign* or *Liahona*, Nov. 2017, 14.

13 Acting in Faith

[1] James E. Faust, "Be Not Afraid," *Ensign*, Oct. 2002, 6.

[2] Boyd K. Packer, "The Edge of the Light," *BYU Magazine*, Mar. 1991, magazine.byu.edu.

Part III: Hearing Him through Dreams, Visions, or Visitations

[1] Jeffrey R. Holland, Twitter post, Mar. 29, 2021, 12:35 p.m., https://twitter.com/hollandjeffreyr/.

14 Heavenly Comfort

[1] "Where Can I Turn for Peace?," *Hymns*, no. 129.

[2] *Hymns*, no. 129.

15 He Parted the Veil

[1] Donald L. Hallstrom, "I *Am* a Child of God," *Ensign* or *Liahona*, May 2016, 27.

[2] Gerrit W. Gong, "Covenant Belonging," *Ensign* or *Liahona*, Nov. 2019, 81.

16 Scars Can Be Reminders of Miracles

[1] Dieter F. Uchtdorf, "Believe, Love, Do," *Ensign* or *Liahona*, Nov. 2018, 47.

17 Eternal Hug

[1] Russell M. Nelson, "Doors of Death," *Ensign*, May 1992, 72.

[2] Jeffrey R. Holland, "The Ministry of Angels," *Ensign* or *Liahona*, Nov. 2008, 29.

[3] Russell M. Nelson, "Doors of Death," 74.

Part IV: Hearing Him through Others

[1] Ronald A. Rasband, "Standing with the Leaders of the Church," *Ensign* or *Liahona*, May 2016, 48.

19 Blessings of Faith

[1] Neil L. Andersen, "The Prophet of God," *Ensign* or *Liahona*, May 2018, 26.

[2] Jeffrey R. Holland, "Behold Thy Mother," *Ensign* or *Liahona*, Nov. 1016, 48.

20 Sweet Bread

[1] Joseph B. Wirthlin, "The Virtue of Kindness," *Ensign* or *Liahona*, May 2005, 26.

[2] Spencer W. Kimball, "Small Acts of Service," *Ensign*, Dec. 1974.

21 He Was Inspired

[1] Dieter F. Uchtdorf, "Your Adventure through Mortality," *Ensign*, March 2019, 25.

[2] Dallin H. Oaks, "The Atonement and Faith," *Ensign* or *Liahona*, Apr. 2010, 30.

22 My Little Son

[1] Gordon B. Hinckley, "God Grant Us Faith," *Ensign*, Nov. 1983, 53.

23 Healing within Little Arms

[1] Dallin H. Oaks, "He Heals the Heavy Laden," *Ensign* or *Liahona*, Nov. 2006, 7.

24 He Was Aware

[1] Larry R. Lawrence, "The War Goes On," *Ensign* or *Liahona*, Apr. 2017, 35.

Part V: Hearing Him When Attending the Temple

[1] Boyd K. Packer, "The Holy Temple," *Ensign*, October 2010, 35.

26 The Sealing Room Was Filled with Light

[1] Becky Craven, Facebook post, Jan. 10, 2020, https://www.facebook.com/YW2ndCounselor/.

[2] Enzio F. Busche, "To the Ends of the Earth," *Ensign*, Feb. 1985.

[3] Myrtle Reed, *Old Rose and Silver* (New York: G.P. Putnam, 1910), 157.

[4] Enzio F. Busche, "To the Ends of the Earth."

[5] Rascal Flatts, "Bless the Broken Road," track 2 on *Feels Like Today*, Lyric Street Records, 2004, compact disc.

27 A Temple Blessing of Peace

[1] Cristina B. Franco, "The Healing Power of Jesus Christ," *Ensign* or *Liahona*, Nov. 2020, 61.

[2] Thomas S. Monson, "The Holy Temple—a Beacon to the World," *Ensign* or *Liahona*, May 2011, 93.

28 Direction in the Temple

[1] Gerrit W. Gong, "Always Remember Him," *Ensign* or *Liahona*, May 2016, 109.

[2] Gary E. Stevenson, "Sacred Homes, Sacred Temples," *Ensign* or *Liahona*, May 2009, 101.

Part VI: Hearing Him When Led to Do Good

[1] Jean B. Bingham, "That Your Joy Might Be Full," *Ensign* or *Liahona*, Nov. 2017, 86.

30 I Can Open My Journal

[1] Michelle D. Craig, "Spiritual Capacity," *Ensign* or *Liahona*, Nov. 2019, 21.

[2] Neil L. Andersen, "Spiritually Defining Memories," *Ensign* or *Liahona*, May 2020, 21.

31 Forgiving Is Hard—Not Forgiving Is Harder

[1] Lysa Terkeurst, *Forgiving What You Can't Forget* (Nashville, Tennessee: Thomas Nelson, 2020), 201.

[2] Terkeurst, *Forgiving What You Can't Forget*, 103–104.

32 We Connected through the Spirit

[1] Henry B. Eyring, "Trust in That Spirit Which Leadeth to Do Good," *Ensign* or *Liahona*, May 2016, 18.

[2] Silvia H. Allred, "Charity Never Faileth," *Ensign* or *Liahona*, Nov. 2011, 116.

[3] M. Russell Ballard, "Joy in Service," *Ensign* or *Liahona*, May 2011, 48.

Part VII: Hearing Him When Healing from Abuse or Mental Illness

[1] Reyna I. Aburto, "The Grave Has No Victory," *Liahona*, May 2021.

33 Lonely but Not Alone

[1] Jeffrey R. Holland, "The Ministry of Reconciliation," *Ensign* or *Liahona*, Nov. 2018, 79.

34 He Was There All Along

[1] Neal A. Maxwell, "But for a Small Moment" (Brigham Young University devotional, Sept. 1, 1974), speeches.byu.edu.

35 The Process of Being Healed

[1] Russell M. Nelson, "Let God Prevail," *Ensign* or *Liahona*, Nov. 2020, 92.

36 My Soul Has Always Known

[1] Reyna I. Aburto, "Thru Cloud and Sunshine, Lord, Abide with Me!," *Ensign* or *Liahona*, Nov. 2019, 58.

[2] Jeffrey R. Holland, "Tomorrow the Lord Will Do Wonders Among You," *Ensign* or *Liahona*, May 2016, 127.

37 Healing and Direction

[1] Dieter F. Uchtdorf, "Move Forward in Faith," *Ensign*, Aug. 2013, 54.

[2] Matthew Holland, "Wrong Roads and Revelation," *New Era*, July 2005, 26.

38 My "Mountains"

[1] "Be Still, My Soul," *Hymns*, no. 124

Part VIII: Hearing Him When Struggling with Addiction

[1] Chieko N. Okazaki, *Lighten Up!* (Salt Lake City: Deseret Book, 1993), 174.

39 Relapse (Almost)

[1] Dieter F. Uchtdorf, "The Hope of God's Light," *Ensign* or *Liahona*, May 2013, 70.

40 He Answered through Someone Else

[1] David A. Bednar, "The Principles of My Gospel," *Liahona*, May 2021.

[2] Dieter F. Uchtdorf, "God among Us," *Liahona*, May 2021, 8.

41 He Is Always Close

[1] David A. Bednar, "Bear Up Their Burdens with Ease," *Ensign* or *Liahona*, May 2014, 90.

42 Courage, Not Compromise

[1] Dale G. Renlund, "Choose You This Day," *Ensign* or *Liahona*, Nov. 2018, 106.

[2] Richard G. Scott, "Personal Strength through the Atonement of Jesus Christ," *Ensign* or *Liahona*, Nov 2013, 83.

[3] Boyd K. Packer, "Worthy Music, Worthy Thoughts," *Ensign*, Apr. 2008, 32.

[4] Thomas S. Monson, "Be Strong and of a Good Courage," *Ensign* or *Liahona*, May 2014, 69.

[5] Bradley R. Wilcox, "Worthiness Is Not Flawlessness," *Liahona*, Nov. 2021, 62.

43 His Eternal Time Line

[1] Susan H. Porter, "God's Love: The Most Joyous to the Soul," *Liahona*, Nov. 2021, 35.

[2] Dallin H. Oaks, "Timing," *Ensign*, Oct. 2003, 12.

44 Sing

[1] "Preface," *Hymns*, x.

45 Rescue in a Song

[1] Jeffery R. Holland, "Songs Sung and Unsung," *Ensign* or *Liahona*, May 2017, 50.

[2] Reuben J. Clark, in Conference Report, Oct. 1936, 111.

[3] Bessel van der Kolk, *The Body Keeps the Score: Brain, Mind, and Body in the Healing of Trauma* (New York City: Viking Press, 2014).

[4] Lauren Daigle, "Rescue," track 2 on *Look Up Child*, Centricity Music, 2018, compact disc.

[5] Ezra Taft Benson, "Do Not Despair," *Ensign*, Nov. 1974, 67.

46 Beyond the Spoken Word

[1] Russell M. Nelson, "The Power and Protection of Worthy Music," *Ensign*, Dec. 2009, 14.

[2] "God Be With You Till We Meet Again," *Hymns*, no. 152.

47 My Refuge

[1] Dieter F. Uchtdorf, "Two Principles for Any Economy," *Ensign* or *Liahona*, Nov. 2009, 58.

[2] Dieter F. Uchtdorf, "The Love of God," *Ensign* or *Liahona*, Nov. 2009, 23.

[3] Kendra Cherry, "What Does the Color Green Mean?" Verywell Mind, July 17, 2022, https://www.verywellmind.com/color-psychology-green-2795817.

[4] Russell M. Ballard, "God's Love for His Children," *Ensign*, May 1988, 59.

48 The Master Gardener

[1] Thomas S. Monson, "Be Your Best Self," *Ensign* or *Liahona*, May 2009, 68.

Part X: Hearing Him in Times of Death, Heartache, or Loss

[1] Jeffrey R. Holland, "For Times of Trouble," *Liahona*, Jan. 1982.

50 I Heard a Voice

[1] Dallin H. Oaks, "Strengthened by the Atonement of Jesus Christ," *Ensign* or *Liahona*, Nov. 2015, 64.

[2] Russell M. Nelson, "Opening Message," *Ensign* or *Liahona*, May 2020, 6.

52 I Closed My Eyes and Opened My Heart

[1] Joseph B. Wirthlin, "Come What May and Love It," *Ensign* or *Liahona*, Nov. 2008, 28.

[2] Henry B. Eyring, "Fear Not to Do Good," *Ensign* or *Liahona*, Nov. 2017, 103.

53 He Caught My Attention

[1] David P. Homer, "Hearing His Voice," *Ensign* or *Liahona*, May 2019, 43.

54 Listening through My Ears, Eyes, Mind, and Heart

[1] Dale G. Renlund, "Consider the Goodness and Greatness of God," *Ensign* or *Liahona*, May 2020, 44.

[2] Dieter F. Uchtdorf, "You Matter to Him," *Ensign* or *Liahona*, Nov. 2011, 22.

[3] Joseph B. Wirthlin, "Come What May and Love It," *Ensign* or *Liahona*, Nov. 2008, 28.

[4] Colin Bates, "5 Listening Insights from the Chinese Character for Listening," SkillPacks, http://www.skillpacks.com/chinese-character-listening-5day-plan/.

Conclusion: From the Authors

[1] Henri Nouwen, "Joy," Henri Nouwen Society, June 1, 2022, https://henrinouwen.org/meditations/joy/.

55 Choose Joy

[1] Dieter F. Uchtdorf, "Grateful in Any Circumstances," *Ensign* or *Liahona*, May 2014, 75.

[2] Joseph B. Wirthlin, "Come What May, and Love it," *Ensign* or *Liahona*, Nov. 2008, 26–28.

[3] Dieter F. Uchtdorf, "The Love of God," *Ensign*, Nov. 2010, 23.

ABOUT THE AUTHORS

Diony Heppler (RN, BSN) has been writing books for over fourteen years. Nonfiction is her favorite genre to write, especially if it helps others become closer to Heavenly Father and the Savior Jesus Christ. She grew up in Alaska but has lived in several other states and overseas. She enjoys traveling, hiking, baking, and spending time with family and friends.

Trent has a BS in business management and is passionate about helping others transform and elevate their lives—what his first book is based on. His career has ranged from management in several businesses and industries to running his own consulting and life coaching company. His extroverted nature fuels his love to connect with others. He was born in Canada but has mostly lived in the northwest part of the United States.

Together they are passionate about hearing and following God, serving, writing, and experiencing life side by side. They have ten children and eight grandchildren, and they currently reside in Kansas City, Missouri.

Scan to visit

Scan to visit

https://www.facebook.com/dionyluvs2write   https://www.trentheppler.com